THE RIGHTS OF WOMEN

THE

RIGHTS OF WOMEN

A Comparative Study in History and Legislation

BY

M. OSTROGORSKI

TRANSLATED UNDER THE AUTHOR'S SUPERVISION

PORCUPINE PRESS

Philadelphia

First edition 1893
(London: Swan Sonnenschein & Co., 1893)

Reprinted 1980 by
PORCUPINE PRESS INC.
Philadelphia, PA 19107

Library of Congress Cataloging in Publication Data

Ostrogorskii, Moisei IAkovlevich, 1854-1919.
The rights of women.

Reprint of the 1893 ed. published by S. Sonnenschein, London, and by Scribner, New York, in the Social science series.
1. Women's rights. 2. Women—Suffrage.
3. Women—Legal status, laws, etc. I. Title.
HQ1236.072 323.3'4 80-21262
ISBN 0-87991-960-4

Manufactured in the United States of America

PUBLISHER'S
PREFACE TO THE ENGLISH EDITION

THE increased importance attaching to the Woman's Rights question throughout the civilised world is no longer a matter of opinion. It could not perhaps be more strongly attested than by the circumstances which gave rise to the publication of this monograph.

The Paris Faculté de Droit opened an international competition for the best essay on the subject, and after the examination of all the works submitted to it, the jury awarded the first prize to M. Ostrogorski, the author of the present volume.

The opinion of the jury was expressed as follows:—
"Il est supérieur à tous les autres. . . . Son œuvre porte l' empreinte d'un esprit robuste qui saisit avec justesse les faits et leurs nuances, et dégage avec une sage modération la signification qu'il faut y attacher pour la marche générale des idées réformatrices. Il expose le sujet sans omettre aucun détail, dans une dissertation vigoureuse, exempte de hors d'œuvre. . . . Le plan n'est pas un instant perdu de vue; la méthode est excellente. . . . Le livre récompensé est un livre

distingué, profondément réfléchi, d'une lecture attachante."

Since the publication of the work in Paris it has been carefully revised and brought up to date by the author, who has rewritten the concluding chapter and added two important Appendices for the English edition.

In examining the part assigned to women in the different elective bodies and public offices, the author has thought it would assist the reader to supply him with the necessary information concerning the character and organisation of each institution. In the opinion of the Publishers this lends an additional value to the monograph, and they do not think any apology is needed for leaving this information exactly as it stands, including that which relates to English-speaking countries. If the ordinary English citizen knows the institutions of his own country, he is, as a rule, imperfectly acquainted with Colonial and American institutions.

The volume is believed to be a unique attempt to collect, and to reduce to a system, all the available information on the subject with which it deals.

TABLE OF CONTENTS

INTRODUCTION.

FROM the very beginning of history woman appears everywhere in a state of complete subordination. Law, which comes to regulate by fixed rules the relations of men in society, sanctions the subjection of woman. At Rome, legislating for the universe, this tenet is formulated in the harshest terms. Christianity, though bringing with it a refining influence, does little to alter woman's position; the Canon Law cannot forgive her the seduction of Adam. "Adam per Evam deceptus est, non Eva per Adam. Quem vocavit ad culpam mulier justum est ut eum gubernatorem assumat ne iterum feminea facilitate labatur."[1] The barbarian society, which rises in the place of the Greco-Roman world, founded as it was on force, shows no greater willingness to recognise the personality of woman; her legal *status* here is one of perpetual tutelage. As social and economic conditions develop and differentiate in the course of the Middle Ages, the unmarried woman gradually liberates herself from the legal restric-

[1] "Adam was beguiled by Eve, not Eve by Adam. It is just that woman should take as her ruler him whom she incited to sin, that he may not fall a second time through female levity." (St. Ambrose quoted in the Decretal; Decret. ii., p. 23, c. 17.)

tions embarrassing her everyday life, that is, in the domain of private law. Then, since the feudal system attaches political power to the patrimonial ownership of the soil, the woman of noble birth, by her ability to inherit, gains access to that power. Before long, however, the territorial sovereignty thus parcelled out becomes reunited and concentrated, with all the political power associated with it, in the hands of the monarch; the confusion between public and private law begins to clear away; and through this double process, *viz.*, in the existing order of things and in men's ideas, woman is in a fair way to be consigned for ever to the region of private law, to the corner left there for her occupation.

But the French Revolution bursts out, and henceforth everything in the State and society is doomed to change. The position of woman, it is true, is not altered at once by the Revolution. Nay, more, it is the French Revolution which puts the final touch to the separation of private from public law; but it does something more than this. It proclaims through the world the reign of "natural right." The sovereign authority of the latter confers on every human being the titles required to support any just claim. Availing oneself of that authority, one could meet, by raising the previous question, all opposition based on the past, on custom, on traditions consecrated by centuries. Then after the "declaration of the rights of man and of the citizen," the declaration of the rights of woman could not fail to come as a logical sequel. It comes and meets with a cold welcome. But, inasmuch as natural right is of eternal validity, are not the claims based on it imprescriptible? So thought, indeed, the champions of woman's rights, and the demand for them is renewed; it crosses first the channel, then the ocean. The agitation in its favour goes on increasing, and by an ever louder clamour forces itself on the public ear. Statesmen and ministers pay it their attention; and the legislator himself begins to bow to it. In the politics of some countries the *rights of women* obtain, for the sake of party game, something like a negotiable value on 'Change, they are quoted, they are speculated upon, by some with hope, by others with dread of their coming before long to rule the market.

Is a change, then, about to pass over the face of the social order? Is political life about to enter on an untrodden path? No mind that busies itself with the future destinies of society can avoid asking itself these questions.

From the indistinct din of the thousand voices ringing in the lists of politics, it would be no easy task to bring out the true answer. We should merely, it is to be feared, catch the voice overpowering for the moment the rest. Opposite, however, to the political arena in which the various tendencies, striving to force themselves upon society, wage their struggle, there is an umpire, well placed for surveying what is going on. That arbiter is the Law. In its threefold aspect of legislation, judicial opinion, and legal doctrine, it watches the contest, marks the blows, but records only such as tell. Prone as it may be to hasty impulses, or still oftener to fits, sometimes prolonged fits, of forgetfulness, it yet traces with much accuracy the salient and inward angles of the curve which the conscience of societies describes in its oscillations.

Then, by examining the laws of the different countries as to the position of woman, with regard to the exercise of political and public rights, one might be able to follow the *woman's rights* movement through its various phases in this and that land, and to perceive the limits provisionally assigned to it by the conscience of the civilised world.

It is this study in history and comparative legislation that I propose to undertake here. I intend to examine, with that special view, every class of political and public rights in turn, from the exercise of the highest power in the State, down to the humblest civic functions.

Several savants and publicists in Europe and in America have been so good as to assist me in my task. Miss Helen Blackburn, editor of the *Englishwoman's Review*, has graciously placed at my disposal her collection of American publications on the subject; M. Aschehong, professor in the University of Christiania; Mr. J. G. Bourinot, LL.D., clerk to the House of Commons in the Canadian Parliament; M. W. Chydenius of the University of Helsingfors; M. Gumplowicz, professor in the University of Graz; M. Hilty, professor in the University of Berne; Dr. Krsnjavi, head of the Public

Worship and Education Department in Croatia; and M. Maurice Vauthier, professor in the University of Brussels, have kindly forwarded translations or analyses of texts, or in other ways supplied me with information as to the legislation of their respective countries; and lastly, Mr. Munroe Smith, professor to the Faculty of Political Science in Columbia College, New York, has done me the great favour of collating and completing my quotations from the legislative enactments on women's school suffrage, in the different States of the American Union. To all these persons I offer my sincerest thanks.

M. O.

RIGHTS OF WOMEN.

CHAPTER I.

Individual Sovereignty.

§ 1.—Succession to the Throne.

So long as sovereignty was a personal dignity, as under the Roman Empire and among the barbarous peoples of the early centuries, woman was of necessity excluded from the succession to the throne. With the Germanic races royalty had above all a military significance. The most intrepid warrior, or the ablest chief, became king. The attachment to certain families—which caused chiefs to be always chosen from them—was not in itself sufficient to place the women of these families in command. At the most they were crowned in the person of their husbands when the male line of these princely families came to an end. Of this we have examples in the Gothic races. When the dynastic order was established, and when the feudal tenure became hereditary instead of personal, the holder of the fief could nominate his daughters to succeed him. The German custom, which in general was hostile to woman, did not interfere in the matters of property and of heredity. The person having no existence proper in the society of that epoch, and social order being summed up in property alone, the claims of land were always weightier than the claims of person. So, in the immense variety of tenures which feudal history presents to us, we shall find several instances of feminine succession. Women exercised to the full the powers that were attached to the land either by proxy, by bailiffs, or in person. They levied troops, held courts of justice, coined money, and took part in the assembly of peers that met at the court of the lord. But with the fourteenth century a reaction set in against female succession to fiefs. In order to stop the frittering away of the principalities which arbitrary patrimonial succession created, a fixed law of heredity was gradually introduced. It was mainly in German territory that the need for this was felt. The general rule established there was male succession and indivisibility of the throne. The Golden Bull of 1356 declared that all the fiefs held immediately of the empire would only be transmissible to male heirs. Anticipating the emergency of the male line becoming extinct, princely houses made a *pactum confraternitatis*, which conferred upon the contracting families, in that contingency, a reciprocal right of succession to their possessions.

Absolute monarchy, that aimed at getting all domains within its grasp, could not be more favourable to female succession; in transmitting their property to their husbands, women formed as it were a centrifugal force as opposed to the concentrating force of monarchy. Hence there was an ever increasing tendency to debar females from succeeding to the throne. But the good pleasure of princes and fatherly affection often caused this rule to be set aside. And the result is, that the present monarchical law which sprung from those actions of personal authority as well as of ancient traditional customs, is very far from showing a uniform system, as regards the succession of women to the crown.

(2) The systems in force in different countries may be classed under three heads:

In certain countries women are absolutely excluded from succeeding to the throne. This is the order of the Salic Law. The prototype of this system is furnished by France where Salic Law first originated. The exclusion of women from the crown was the custom in that country ever since the kings of the first dynasty. Under the feudal system, it is true, there were several female fiefs, but in the *Ile de France* male succession was at all times absolute. Proportionately as fiefs became merged in the kingdom of France, this rule gained wider application, and finally became public law in the monarchy. Known by the name of the Salic Law, it had its basis less in a written document[1] than in the general conception of woman as an inferior being. "The kingdom of France," said Froissart, "is of such great nobility, that it must not be suffered to pass by succession to the female."[2] "The daughters of France," so Dutillet explains, "are perpetually debarred from the crown by custom and by

[1] As we know, the name Salic Law really belongs to a code of procedure and of private and penal law wherein not the slightest mention is made of the rights of succession to the throne.

[2] Book I., chap. xxii.

a special law of the house of France founded on the pride of the French, who could not bear to be ruled by their own women folk."[1] In 1316 Philippe le Long, when succeeding his brother, Louis le Hutin, had, for a while, to defend his right to the throne against his niece, but the claim made on her behalf was rejected. Twelve years later a similar dispute had more serious results, for it brought about the Hundred Years' War. Edward, King of England, while admitting the exclusion of women from the throne, did not consider that this law touched their male descendants, and, as he was a nearer male relative of the late king than Philippe of Valois, he maintained that it was to him, Edward, that the crown belonged. From this long, bloody war, Salic Law emerged victoriously. It was again called in question during the troubled period previous to the Bourbon succession; with Henry IV. its triumph was final. Perhaps the decision of the Paris Parliament of June 28th, 1593, declaring any arrangement "made to the prejudice of the Salic Law," to be null and void, had also some weight in the decision.

On the eve of the Revolution, when there arose the famous question which occasioned such floods of ink, *viz.*, "if France had a Constitution," the Salic Law was cited as one of the articles of this "Constitution." The Parliament of Paris, eager to have its say, believed that it had discovered seven articles in the aforesaid Constitution, and in 1787 it set these forth as follows:—

"The Parliament of Paris declares that France is a

[1] "Recueil des rois de France," chap. i., p. 308. Cited by Laboulage, "Recherches sur la condition civile et politique des femmes." Paris, 1843.

monarchy governed by a king according to the laws; and that of these laws several fundamental ones comprehended and sanctioned, first, The right of the reigning house to the throne from male to male in the order of primogeniture. Second, The right of the nation freely to grant subsidies by the agency of the States General. . . . Seventh, The Court (the Parliament) protests against any violation of the principles here laid down."

It was the *Constituante* Assembly that first gave the sanction of written law to the Salic custom. The question gave rise to no doubts. When at the sitting of August 27th, 1789, it was proposed in the National Assembly to discuss the articles relative to the monarchy, it was remarked "that they already existed in the minds of all Frenchmen, and it was impossible to resist the evidence of these principles." Pétion added that "among the articles there were many of evident utility to the French people and their peace, such as the maintenance of the monarchy, the male succession to the throne, the exclusion of females."[1] At the evening sitting of the same date, Mounier read Chapter II. of the project of the Constitution, one of the articles of which stated: "The crown is indivisible and hereditary, from branch to branch, from male to male, and by order of primogeniture. Females and their descendants are excluded."[2] On Sept. 15th, 1789, "the National Assembly unanimously declared as fundamental laws of the French Monarchy, that the person of the King is sacred and inviolable, that the throne is indivisible, that

[1] Reprint of the old "Moniteur." P. 1850, t. I., p. 387.

[2] *Ibid*, p. 390.

the crown is hereditary to the reigning house from male to male in order of primogeniture and to the perpetual and absolute exclusion of women."[1] In the final text of the Constitution of 1791, these provisions were inserted in Title iii., chap. ii., sec. 1, art. 1. The Imperial Constitutions of 1804, 1852, and 1870, reproduced them. On the other hand, the Constitutional Charters of 1814, of the Bourbon Restoration, and of 1830, of the Orleans Monarchy, omitted to state the order of the succession to the throne.

The other countries governed by Salic Law in all its rigour are Belgium, Italy, the Scandinavian kingdoms, Luxemburg, and Roumania. The fundamental laws of these monarchies expressly state that women and their descendants are excluded from the throne. The Italian Constitution briefly points out that "the throne is hereditary in conformity with the conditions of the Salic Law." It was by the application of this law that Luxemburg became some years ago detached from the kingdom of the Netherlands. This Grand Duchy became connected with Holland, in 1815, by the personal union of the Orange-Nassau Dynasty. But from time immemorial there prevailed in Luxemburg the custom of male succession, which has been formally recognised by the Succession Union of the Nassau family of June 30th, 1783. The treaty of Vienna of 1815, and that of London of 1867, both stipulated that the rights of males to the succession of the Grand Duchy should be maintained. The Constitution of 1868 acknowledged it (Art. 3), and when the King-Grand Duke William III. was succeeded in 1890 by his daughter, Wilhelmina, the

[1] *Ibid*, p. 471.

bonds which bound Luxemburg to the Netherlands were lawfully broken, and the Duchy passed to the nearest of kin of the other branch of the House of Nassau.

(4) According to the second system, the female succession is admitted, but only in a subsidiary form, that is to say, the crown passes to women in default of male heirs to the reigning house. It is thus that the order of succession is established in Austria, in most of the German states, and in Greece.

The Austrian order of succession was established by the famous "Pragmatische sanction" of the Emperor Charles VI., in 1713, which admitted to the throne, in default of male heirs, the daughters (arch-duchesses) of the late emperor, passing over the heads of princesses of the elder branches.

The existing laws in the kingdom of Prussia are somewhat obscure. Art. 53 of the Constitution declares that, "in conformity with the laws of the Royal House, the crown passes to male heirs in the order of primogeniture and in direct lineal succession." In default of all male heirs, are women excluded or not? Upon this point the Constitution is dumb, and only stipulates for the order of succession to be observed "in the male line," while it does not state whether that line is the only one qualified for the crown. Nor do the laws of the Royal House (Hausgesetze) solve the question; they merely point to an incontestable preference for male succession. Commentators on Prussian law are divided in their interpretation of these texts. While Zachariæ, Grotefend and Schulze[1] consider women to be perpetually excluded

[1] Schulze, "Das Staatsrecht des Kœnigreichs Preussen," p. 48. Freiburg, 1884 (Collection of "Handbuch des œffentlichen Rechts," edit. by Prof. Marquardsen.)

from succession to the throne, von Held, Zoepfl, and Roenne[1] refuse to admit this, alleging the absence of any express statement as to the incapacity of women. The first opinion is based upon the logical interpretation of the texts: if Art. 53, dealing with possible heirs to the throne, only speaks of males, that is because it intends to reserve to them the exclusive right of succession, *qui de uno dicit de altero negat.* But on the other hand, the common law of Germany having, as a general rule, for centuries, allowed to women a subsidiary right to the succession of the throne, there is no sufficient reason for their exclusion in the fact that the articles of the Constitution omit to specify this. The controversy, however, is not of great practical importance, owing to the Fraternal Pacts which bind the House of Prussia to those of Saxony and Hesse, and which ensure male sovereigns to Prussia in the event of the extinction of the Hohenzollerns.

The Constitutions of Bavaria, Saxony, and Würtemberg, expressly state that in default of male successors, the crown shall pass to women. Bavarian law even allows for the succession of a princess married to a foreign sovereign, only imposing the necessity of appointing a viceroy for Bavaria, who shall reside in the kingdom; after this princess, the throne passes to her second son. The law of Baden admits the succession of the female line, but not persons of the female sex, so that the throne would go to sons of a princess, but not to the princess herself.

With regard to the Imperial throne of Germany, no

[1] L. v. Rœnne, "Das Staatsrecht der Preussischen Monarchie," 4th Edition, v. i., p. 168.

special laws of succession exist; by virtue of the Constitution of the Empire (Art. 11), the Imperial dignity belongs by right to the monarch who occupies the throne of Prussia.

The order of succession to the throne of Greece is regulated by Art. 45 of the Constitution ("the preference being in favour of male heirs," irrespective of lines).

(5) Finally, the third system of heredity to the throne is where women possess a right to succeed to the throne concurrently with males (*successio promiscua*). This system obtains in Spain, Portugal, England, Russia, and Holland.

This order of succession was once termed the Castilian Law, and it is in the modern Constitutions of Spain and Portugal that we find it set forth in a general manner. Art. 60 of the Spanish Constitution is in the following terms:—

"The succession to the throne is to occur in the regular order of primogeniture and by representation, the anterior line always being preferred to the posterior; in the same line, the nearer degree shall be preferred to that more remote, and in the same degree, the male to the female, and, as regards age, the older to the younger."

Applying this rule to the actual reigning dynasty of Spain, Art. 61 of the Constitution determines that when the lines of legitimate descendants of King Alphonso XII. shall become extinct, his sisters shall succeed, then his aunt, sister of his mother, and finally his uncles, the brothers of Don Ferdinand VII., if they are not excluded. But it is precisely the legitimacy of this order of succession which the descendants of these "uncles," to wit, Don Carlos, dispute; they pretend that the real law of succession to the Spanish throne is the Salic Law. Such a protest is, as we know, not limited to theoretical controversy; for more than half a century it has constituted a permanent menace to political stability in Spain, and from time to time it has produced sanguinary outbursts (*Carlist* insurrections) which have plunged the kingdom into all the horrors of civil war.

From a legal point of view, the dispute is based upon the following facts. In written confirmation of the ancient custom of the peninsula, Alfonso X. caused it to be inscribed in the famous book of *las siete partidas* (which appeared in 1260) that the succession to the throne should always pass in a direct line, and if there were no male child, the eldest daughter should succeed (law 2 of title xv. of the 2nd *partida*).[1] Philip V. abolished this order of succession, and adopted the agnatic succession. This Act, inserted in the *Autos Accordados,* lib. v., tit. 7., auto. v. (May 10th, 1713), became the fundamental law of the kingdom. The Cortes of 1789, in response to the wish of Charles IV., proposed to abrogate the *Auto Accordado* of Philip V., and to go back to the immemorial custom of the *siete partidas.* The King accepted, but exacted from the Cortes absolute secrecy until the moment of promulgation. This, however, did not take place during Charles IV.'s reign. The Constitution of 1812, it is true, proclaimed a return to the law of *siete partidas,* but the Constitution itself had only a short life. With the restoration of Ferdinand VII. to the throne, the old order

[1] The best account of the old order of succession in Spain is still that given by Mignet in the Collection of unpublished documents on the history of France, "Negociations relatives à la succession d'Espagne, t. i."

of things was re-established. At length, in 1830, Ferdinand VII., who left an only daughter as his heir, promulgated the Act of 1789; but his brother, Don Carlos, disputed this on the grounds that the King had no right, after forty years, to enforce a law that was still-born and had never been sanctioned. Three years later, by virtue of this law, Isabella II. succeeded to the throne, but the partisans of Carlos took up arms in defence of the *Auto Accordado* of 1713. The Constitution of 1876, as we have remarked, sanctioned the admission of women, but the Carlists always contest the legitimacy of such sanction.

In Portugal, the fitness of women to succeed to the throne is recognised by Art. 87 of the Constitution, couched in terms identical with those of Art. 60 of the Spanish Constitution.

(6) The texts of English constitutional law do not contain formal provisions as to the order of succession to the throne. The Act of Settlement of June 12th, 1701, only ensures the crown to descendants of the Princess Sophia of Hanover. Hereditary succession to the throne is regulated by common law. The lines followed are the same as those for the succession to property, with a slight modification,[1] which is akin to the system

[1] According to the rule of the Common Law, which is itself derived from the feudal system, the succession of daughters does not follow the rule of primogeniture, but they all inherit the estate as coparceners, for, as Blackstone explains, being all equally incapable of performing any personal service, and therefore one main reason for preferring the eldest not applying, such preference would be injurious to the rest. However, the succession by primogeniture, even among females, takes place as to inheritance of the crown; wherein the necessity of a sole and determinate succession is as

which, as we have just seen, exists in the Iberian peninsula. And this is, that if in the same line there are no male heirs, the succession reverts to the eldest of the princesses, although there may be princes of younger lines. It is thus that Queen Victoria succeeded her uncle, William IV., who left no issue, but who had two younger brothers, the Duke of Kent and the Duke of Cumberland. The Duke of Kent having predeceased William IV., his daughter, Victoria, as representing the elder line, took precedence over the Duke of Cumberland. It is the most recent, but by no means a unique instance of a woman succeeding to the crown of England. Not to mention the illustrious Queen Elizabeth, several of her sex have worn the British crown, *viz.*, Mary Tudor, Mary, daughter of James II., and Anne, her niece. Mary Tudor induced the Parliament to vote that a queen should enjoy absolutely the same rights as a king. The Parliament did not grudge her the Bill asked for,[1] because royal power, even as enjoyed by males, was in England considerably limited. Upon the accession of Elizabeth, Aylmer, afterwards Bishop of London, in confuting Knox's

great in the one sex as in the other (Stephen's Commentaries on the Laws of England, founded on Blackstone, 11th edit., L., 1890, vol. i., pp. 389-391).

[1] Mar. sess. iii., c. i., declares "the rights of the queen to be so clear that none but the malitious and ignorant could be induced and persuaded unto this Errour and Folly, to think that her Highness coulde ne shoulde have, enjoye, and use suche lyke Royall Aucthoritie . . . nor doo ne execute and use all thinges concerning the statutes as the kings of this Realm her most noble progenitours have heretofore doon, enjoyed and exercised" (Statutes at large, vi., 18).

protest against female government,[1] stated: "It is not in England so dangerous a matter to have a woman ruler, as men take it to be. For, first, it is not she that ruleth, but the laws, the executors whereof be her judges. Secondly, she maketh no statutes or laws, but the honourable court of Parliament."[2]

(7) If, according to this doctrine, it is constitutional government which in England has permitted women to rule, in Russia the same result has been achieved by autocratic government. When, for State reasons, Peter the Great violently put his own son beyond the reach of the throne, he declared that monarchs were absolute masters to dispose of the crown as they liked.[3] There being no fixed rules for succession, palace revolutions placed women upon the throne, after the great Emperor's death, for nearly three-quarters of a century. When finally the order of succession was regulated by a statute (in 1797), the right of women to the throne was expressly recognised. Art. 5 of the fundamental laws of the Russian Empire states that "both sexes have a right to succeed to the throne, but this right belongs by preference to males in the order of primogeniture." The law then determines the order of female succession in a very detailed but rather obscure manner. The pith of it amounts to this, that, so long as in the same line there are male heirs, direct descendants of male sove-

[1] Knox assailed female government in a work entitled, "Blast of the Trumpet against the Monstrous Regiment of Women," which was directed against the former Queen Mary.

[2] Hallam, "The Constitutional History of England," 7th edit., in 3 volumes (L., 1854), t. i., p. 281.

[3] Law of 5th February, 1722.

reigns, the males absolutely exclude the females. In default of the said males, the crown first passes to the cognate descendants of the last emperor, secondly to those of his sons, and thirdly to those of his daughters, the male branch being always preferred to the female; but in the branch itself, males only exclude females in the same degree, so that a younger brother would exclude his elder sister, but the elder sister, if not married, would exclude the sons of her younger sister, to cite the instance given in Art. 12 of the fundamental laws.

The fundamental law of the Netherlands, revised in 1887, fixes the order of female succession in the same way as the Russian statute.[1] Thus these two countries assign to woman a lower place than in Spain, Portugal, or England, where if there are no male heirs in the first degree who are entitled, females can succeed to the throne. In the empire of Muscovy, however, and in the kingdom of the Netherlands, they cannot succeed until all male heirs, from male to male, are extinct. An instance of this occurred in Holland at the decease of King William IV., in 1890.

§ 2.—Regency.

Regency is a substitute for Royalty, where the minority or the ill-health of the monarch prevents his discharging his duties. The method of appointment is threefold: (1) by the King's testamentary appointment or other-

[1] In default of male descendants from son to son, the crown passes to the daughters of the last king, and after them to the daughters of his male, and then of his female descendants (Art. 11-15).

wise; (2) by rightful devolution on members of the Royal family in the order settled by the fundamental laws; (3) by the choice of Parliament made in each particular case. The order here given marks the successive phases of the development of that institution; at first the Regency by the King's nomination, coming down from the time when patrimonial estates were held subject to the pleasure of the sovereign; then the fixed order removed from the pleasure of the King but given over to the chance of birth; and lastly, the delegation to a political magistracy by the representatives of national sovereignty. The first-named system of monarchical law, which has lasted for a long while, and has not yet wholly disappeared, was most favourable to women. It allowed them to succeed to the regency even in countries like France where the Salic Law was in force. Regency being only a temporary delegation of the powers of sovereignty, the admission of women did not raise the same objections as when the question was one of the permanent occupation of the throne. Their exclusion from the succession to the throne was indeed a reason for conferring upon them the Regency. As the female Regent could not aspire to the throne under the Salic Law, there was no fear that she would supplant the legitimate sovereign; not to reckon on maternal affection, which alone should be sufficient to prevent her from any wrongful attempt against the infant King. Thus in the hands of a woman, the guardianship of the crown was doubly safe. The Queen-mother, as legal guardian for her son, combined by right the guardianship of the infant with the trust of his property, and of his kingdom as well. It was only when the French Revolution put an end to the existing confusion between public and private law that a distinction was drawn between the guardianship of the King and the governing of his kingdom. This led to the restriction of the rights of women Regents.

(2) In France, under the *ancien régime*, female Regents were not looked upon with disfavour, their total reaching 24, or 1 sister, 2 grandmothers, and 21 mothers. There was no fundamental law calling them to the Regency.[1] Being usually appointed by their husbands, female Regents often found their power disputed by male relatives or by the nobles of the kingdom. They generally ruled with the aid of a council appointed with the object of either supplementing the female Regent's inexperience or of allowing different factions to be represented in the Government. Under absolute monarchy there was no longer any council associated with the female Regent. The Parliament of Paris screened by its authority that change; it even cancelled the will of Louis XIII., which provided Queen Anne with a council, and appointed the Duke of Orléans *lieutenant-général* of the realm.

It was the *Constituante* that, by an organic law, settled the question of the Regency. It separated the latter from the office of guardian, the mother of the infant

[1] Among the different documents we have on this subject, the most important is the edict of Charles VI., proclaimed on 26th December, 1407. It declared that Kings during their minority should govern subject to the good advice, deliberations, and counsels of their Queen-mothers, and of the nearest of kin of the blood royal, and also subject to the deliberations and counsels of the Constables and the Chancellor of France and other discreet men (see the documents published in the appendix to "Précis historique des régences en France," par Dufau and Solar. Paris, 1842).

Sovereign being appointed guardian, while the Regency was bestowed on a male relative of the King, the nearest in order of heredity. Women were expressly debarred from this office. The question formed the subject of a debate in the Assembly. When submitting the Bill for the Regency of the realm, Thouret said in his report:—

"As it is not in the private interest of the King and of his family that the nation has delegated to them hereditary Royalty, so also it is not in the interest of the minor King that a Regent is appointed; neither is the Regency a right inherent in the family. It is herein that this office differs essentially from that of guardian, this latter being solely in the interest of the minor, whereas the Regency is a magistrature instituted in the interest of the people. . . The committee propose to delegate the Regency in a direct line to the eldest and nearest male relative. . . It is futile to set forth reasons for the absolute exclusion of women from the Regency; you have already expressly decreed that they be debarred from succeeding to the crown. . ."

However, the rights of women to the Regency found defenders in the Extreme Right of the *Constituante*, among whom were the Abbé Maury, Cazalès, and others. In an impassioned speech, the Abbé Maury quoted examples from the past: "It may be imprudent," he remarked, "to nominate perpetually the mothers of Kings as Regents, but is there not also some difficulty created by their perpetual exclusion? A custom confirmed by so many precedents deserves particular respect, and it would need most powerful reasons to warrant its repeal by law. . . . The will of the nation should never be fettered.[1] . . ." This speech made but little impression. "The Salic Law," remarked Clermont-Tonnerre, when the question was again discussed at the next sitting, "the Salic Law, which excludes women from the throne, would also seem to prevent their temporarily occupying it. Moreover, long experience has taught us what ill-doing, injustice and weakness usually result from such rule." Thouret vigorously opposed the appeal to precedent in favour of women, remarking: "Former custom does not establish a claim; principles and reason should guide us, and these both exclude women from the Regency." Despite the intervention of Cazalès, the Assembly decreed that women be excluded from the Regency. At the same time it adopted the following measures: "The Regency of the realm confers no right whatever upon the person of the King when a minor." "The guardianship of the King during his minority is to devolve upon his mother, and if he have no mother, or she be married again at the time of her son's accession, or if she should re-marry during his minority, this guardianship is to be delegated by the legislative body, but not to the Regent and his issue nor to women." While clearly defining the principles of public law, these articles of the Constitution satisfied all legitimate interests. The risks to which a boy monarch was exposed during the Regency of an interested person, were prevented at the outset by the clauses protecting the minor from the influence of the Regent or of his family; while at the same time the rights and duties of maternal tenderness were allowed full scope.

The Constitution of 1804 (the *sénatus consulte organi-*

[1] "Moniteur," t. vii. Sitting of 22nd March, 1791.

que of the 20th *floréal*, year XII.), maintained the exclusion of women from the Regency; but that of the 5th February, 1813, went back to the old system. It stated that: "In case the Emperor when a minor should succeed without his father having disposed of the Regency of the Empire, the Empress-mother is entitled to be the guardian of her son and Regent of the Empire." The powers of such a Regent were limited by a council; and, to preserve these intact, she was not allowed to marry again (Art. 2).

The Constitutional Charter of 1814 and that of 1830 contained no references to the Regency. The unfortunate death of the Duke of Orleans, the eldest son and heir apparent of the King Louis Philippe, drew attention to this deficiency, and by a law of August 30th, 1842, it was determined that "the Regency should belong to the prince who was nearest to the throne in the order of succession" (Art. 2). Consequently this meant the exclusion of women. Art. 6 of the same law appointed as the Sovereign's guardian the Queen-mother if she did not re-marry, and failing her, the Queen or Princess, his paternal grandmother, if she had remained a widow.

The second Empire, by the *sénatus consulte* of July 17th, 1856, took up again the *sénatus consulte* of 1813, which in default of a Regent appointed by the infant Emperor's father, invested the Empress-mother with the guardianship as well as with the Regency. It was under female Regency that the Empire, the last monarchical *régime*, ended in France, in 1870. The Emperor Napoleon III., leaving for the seat of war, appointed the Empress Eugénie Regent.

(3) In countries where the Regency is bestowed by

right upon the relative of the infant sovereign (as in Spain, Portugal, Russia,[1] Italy, the German States, Austria, and Luxemburg), women are sometimes excluded and sometimes admitted under diverse conditions. In Spain, Portugal, and Russia,[2] where females succeed to the throne concurrently with males, they obtain the Regency under the same conditions. As to the two countries of the above mentioned, where the Salic law prevails, Regency is strictly agnate in Luxemburg; while in Italy it devolves by preference upon agnates, but in default of males capable of assuming the Regency, it reverts to the Queen-mother. Finally, in Austria and in the German States, where cognates possess a subsidiary right to the crown, their condition is a less favourable one for exercising the functions of Regency. In Austria, Prussia, Saxony, Hesse, and Mecklenburg, Regency is agnate. In Bavaria, Würtemberg, and some small principalities like Oldenburg and Brunswick, in default of agnates the Regency is bestowed upon women in the following order:—In Bavaria, if the Regent has not been nominated by the King, and in default of agnates capable of assuming

[1] In Russia, as in Bavaria and Austria, the Regency is in the first place by appointment.

[2] Articles 67 and 71 of the Spanish Constitution (the Regency belongs to the father and mother of the King, and in their default to the ascendant who is nearest in succession to the crown); Article 92 of the Portuguese Constitution (the Regency is conferred on the ascendant of the King nearest in succession to the throne. In default of heirs the Regent is nominated by the Cortes; and meanwhile the government is conducted by a provisional Regent under the presidency of the widowed Queen); Article 23 of the Russian fundamental laws (provisions similar to the Spanish Constitution).

the Regency, this reverts to the Queen-dowager. Taken literally, this does not make it a *sine quâ non* that the Regent be the mother of the King minor. It is sufficient that she be the widow of the last King; on the other hand, it is not enough for the Princess to be the mother of the King minor if her husband have not been King. In Würtemberg, in default of agnates, the Regency is conferred upon the Queen-mother, and, failing her, upon the paternal grandmother of the King. The same order holds good for the Grand Duchy of Oldenburg and the Duchy of Brunswick.

As regards the Empire of Germany, the rules framed for Prussia apply to the Empire also, the Imperial crown being indissolubly attached to the kingdom of Prussia.

(4) In England,[1] Holland, Sweden and Norway, Denmark, Belgium, Roumania, Servia, and Greece,[2] the Regency is not acquired by right. In these countries, whenever a King is prevented from governing by minority or by illness, a special law, made *ad hoc*, provides for a Regency. In such cases can it be delegated to women?

The fundamental laws of the monarchies just mentioned, while leaving the choice of a Regent to the Legislative body, for the most part make no special mention of the sex of the person to be nominated to the Regency. It is only the Danish law of February 11th, 1871, which requires that the Regent shall be of the male sex. Then the law of 1810 relating to the order of succession in Sweden contains a vague and incomplete reference

[1] See "The English Constitution," by G. Bowyer, L. 1841, p. 207, on the rules established by precedents in England.

[2] In Greece the Regency rendered necessary by the King's minority is conferred by a special law, if the last King has not nominated a Regent.

thereto when it states that "daughters of the Royal House and their heirs, though male, have no right to the crown *nor to the government* of Sweden." The laws of other countries are absolutely silent upon the subject. In the absence of positive texts, the order established for the succession to the throne ought to be the order to be applied to a Regency. If women are excluded from the throne, to allow them to occupy it even temporarily would be contrary to the fundamental rules of public law in the country. But where women are able to succeed to the throne, there is nothing abnormal in its being temporarily confided to their care. And precedent is in favour of this solution. Thus, in England and Holland, which allow of the *successio promiscua*, women have been admitted to the Regency. Under George II. in England, the Dowager-Princess of Wales was eventually nominated Regent; the Duchess of Kent was nominated to fulfil the same functions should her daughter, the future Queen Victoria, accede to the throne when a minor. Neither of those princesses had the opportunity of discharging the duties of Regent. In the Netherlands the law of August 2nd, 1884, appointed Queen Emma Regent of the realm during her widowhood in case of the minority of the successor to the throne. In 1890 this law had occasion to be enforced.

CHAPTER II.

Collective Sovereignty.

THE exercise of supreme power no longer belongs exclusively to princes, but emanates from the nation either by itself or joined to representatives of historic dynasties. In other words, sovereignty has become collective instead of individual. Its direct exercise by the whole body of citizens being impossible, it becomes necessary to delegate it to mandatories, so that collective sovereignty consists practically in the right of sharing in the election of representatives at the national assemblies, and in being qualified for such a mandate.

In the enjoyment of these rights, what is the condition of woman? Almost everywhere she is excluded. The female political vote is still nothing more than a claim. The attempts to secure it by legislation, or by putting a wider construction on the law already in existence, have signally failed except in one or two unimportant cases. A rapid review of such attempts, more especially of those in the domain of judicature, will clearly show the legal position in which women are placed with regard to political suffrage.

§ 1.—FRANCE.

(1) In the preceding chapter I pointed out that in the Middle Ages women of noble birth were not ab-

solutely excluded from political power. Apart from dynastic sovereignty in the proper sense of the term, which could suitably apply only to great fiefs, the heredity of feudal tenures conferred upon women the prerogatives of public power in a considerable number of small signiories. Later, in the elections to the States General, we shall find examples of women of the lower classes taking part in electoral assemblies.[1] Under absolute monarchy the question of woman's political rights could never arise, but through the *salon* and the alcove she soon rose to be a power in the State. In the eighteenth century woman is "the principle that governs, the reason that directs, the voice that commands. She is the universal, fatal cause, the origin of events, the source of things. . . . From one end of the century to the other, the government of woman is the sole government to be seen and felt, having the steadiness of purpose and the spring, the reality and the activity of power." (De Goncourt, "La femme au XVIIIe siécle," p. 372.) But she in no wise sought legal sanction of her power; nor was this claimed for her. In the great crusade for the recognition of unacknow-

[1] So in the register of the towns which sent deputies to the States of Tour in 1308, there are mentioned, for Ferriéres near Beaulieu (in Touraine), several men and women on their own behalf, and also on behalf of the Church (Boutaric, "La France sous Philippe le Bel," p. 444. App.).

Again, at the elections to the States General of 1560 and 1576, widows and daughters holding separate property took part in the assemblies which met to draw up a list of grievances and to choose delegates to present it at the headquarters of the castle ward (A. Babeau, *The representation of the third estate at the assemblies of the third estate for drawing up customs*, "Revue Historique," 1883, t. xxi., p. 95).

ledged rights, in which the eighteenth century philosophers engaged, no attention was paid to the condition of women in the State. The illustrious precursors of the Revolution, who were the spiritual guides of the age, would not admit that woman was fitted for any *rôle* but that of private life. Not only did Montesquieu express his opinion that "nature had given woman accomplishments, and intended that her ascendency should not spread beyond them,"[1] but Rousseau himself declared that woman was specially created in order to please man.[2]

On the eve of the Revolution, however, a great voice arose in favour of the political emancipation of women. The voice was that of Condorcet. He could not see why the benefits of rights recently secured for humanity should not extend to the female portion of it. In his *Lettres d'un Bourgeois de New Haven à un Citoyen de Virginie* (1787), the illustrious thinker wrote: "We would have a constitution, the principles of which are solely founded on the *natural* rights of man previous to social institutions." "One of these rights we consider to be that of voting for common interests either personally or by freely elected representatives. Is it not in their character of sensible beings, capable of reason and with moral ideas, that men have rights? Women, therefore, should have absolutely the same. . . . . Either no individual member of the human race has any real rights, or else all have the same; and whoever votes against the rights of another, no matter what his religion, his colour or his sex may

[1] "Esprit des Lois," lib. xvi., chap 2.

[2] "Emile," lib. v.

be, has henceforth abjured his own." "Finally, you will doubtless admit the principle of the English, that one is legitimately subject only to those taxes for which one has voted, if not personally, at least through the medium of representatives; and from this principle it follows that every woman is entitled to refuse to pay parliamentary taxes. I see no valid reply to such reasoning, at least on the part of widows or unmarried women. As regards the others, one may say that the exercise of a citizen's rights presupposes that an individual may act according to his own free will. But then, I reply, that civil laws which establish between men and women an inequality so great as to suppose the latter deprived of the advantage of having a free will would only constitute another injustice. . ."[1]

This page of Condorcet's contains all the claims and all the arguments with which the battle of woman's political emancipation will be fought in the different countries of the world. There will be nothing added to it, and nothing taken away.

(2) In 1789, at election time, several pamphlets appeared demanding the admission of women to the States General, and protesting against the holding of a national assembly, from which half the nation was excluded. But the number of those writers who claimed for woman not political, but social, equality, and, above all, a reform in her education, was still greater.[2] With one or two exceptions

[1] *Œuvres complètes*, Paris, 1804., xii., 19-21. The same ideas are expressed in an article published on 3rd July, 1790, in the *Journal de la Société de 1789* under the title of "The admission of women to citizen rights."

[2] Ch. L. Chassin, "Le génie de la Révolution," P. 1863, t. i., p. 299. See also "Les cahiers de Paris en 1789," published under

the *cahiers* of the States General contain no mention of the political rights of women. When women themselves make their voices heard, it is always to ask for an improvement in their material condition. In a women's petition to the King they ask "that men may not ply the trades belonging to women, whether dressmaking, embroidery, or haberdashery. Let them leave us, at least, the needle and the spindle, and we will engage not to wield the compass or the square. We desire to be enlightened, to have employments, not in order to usurp men's authority, but that we may be more valued, and have the means of livelihood if overtaken by misfortune."[1] But ere long women grew bolder; the frenzy of the Revolution gave them courage; they demanded equality, full equality, nothing but equality.[2] Upon the "Declaration of the Rights of the Man and the Citizen," Olympe de Gouges published the "Declaration of the Rights of Women," which is a curious *pasticcio* of the former manifesto: "Woman is free born and legally man's equal. The principle of all sovereignty resides essentially in the nation, which is only the

the auspices of the Municipal Council of Paris, in 1889, by Ch. L. Chassin, t. ii., p. 596.

[1] Cited in "Le Socialisme pendant la Révolution," by A. Lefaure, p. 122.

[2] In the petition of the ladies to the National Assembly, they lay on the table a bill containing the following provisions. (1) All privileges of the male sex to be entirely and irrevocably done away with throughout France; (2) The female sex to enjoy the same liberty, the same advantages, the same rights, and the same honours as the male sex; (3) the masculine gender no longer to be regarded, even in a grammatical sense, as the nobler species, seeing that all species and all beings ought to be and are equally noble; (4) . . . (*ibid.*, p. 140).

union of the woman and the man. Liberty and justice consist in restoring all that belongs to others. Thus the exercise of the natural rights of woman has no limits but the perpetual tyranny opposed to it by man. . . . The law should be the same for all. All male and female citizens, being equal in the eyes of the law, ought to be equally admissible to all dignities, posts, and public appointments, according to their capacity, and with no distinctions other than those of their virtues and their talents. . . Woman has the right to mount the scaffold; she should equally have the right to mount the tribune."[1]

The *Constituante* Assembly, however, was not to be persuaded. It only paid women the somewhat platonic compliment of confiding "the depôt of the Constitution to the vigilance of wives and mothers." If in the ranks of the Assembly there were some illustrious or notable men willing to free women from their social and political subjection, like Sieyès, the Abbé Faucher, and others, the great majority would not hear of women's political rights. Men so divergent in their opinions as Mirabeau and Robespierre met together at this point. The former, in a great speech on public education, which he had written and was going to deliver when struck by death, expressed himself as follows:—

"Man and woman play an entirely different part in nature, and they could not play the same part in the social state; the eternal fitness of things only made them move towards one common goal by assigning to them

[1] I have taken the text of the Declaration from the documents which form an appendix to Daniel Sterne's "Histoire de la Revolution de 1848," t. ii., p. 379 (3 vol. edition).

distinct and separate places. . . . To take these modest beings whose maidenly reserve gives a charm to the domestic circle, where all their loveable qualities expand to perfection; to place them among men and affairs; to expose them to the perils of a life which they cannot learn to support except by distorting their physical constitution; this is but to obliterate that exquisite sensibility which, so to speak, constitutes their essence, and becomes the guarantee of their aptitude for the fulfilment of those private functions which a good social scheme has assigned to them. It is to confound everything; it is by vain prerogatives to flatter them into losing sight of those advantages by which they might beautify their existence; it is to degrade them in our eyes and in their own; it is, in a word, to promise them sovereignty and rob them of their empire. No doubt, women ought to reign, but on the hearth, in the home, she should reign there, and there only; everywhere else she is out of place."[1]

The grotesque and somewhat dismal part played by woman under the Terror only too well justified the language of Mirabeau. Having flung themselves into the Revolution with an ardour and an enthusiasm not devoid of grandeur at the outset, they soon lost all balance, intellectual and moral. The Terrorists themselves were disgusted in the end, if not by their excesses, at least by the habit into which they fell, of exciting the people, of remonstrating with the men in office, and of promoting disorder in the streets. Upon the defeat of the Girondins, the Montagnards were not slow in getting

[1] "Travail sur l'Education publique," du Comte de Mirabeau, found among his papers, and published by Cabanis. (P. 1791.)

rid of their sinister allies. On the 28th brumaire, 1793, when a band of red-capped viragoes forced their way into the lobby of the Communal Council-chamber, Chaumette, the *procureur général,* apostrophised them in the severest terms. "What! shall these degraded beings who have shaken off and violated Nature's laws, be suffered to enter a place entrusted to the guardianship of citizens? Since when have women been allowed to abjure their sex and turn themselves into men?"[1] A few days later Amar, in the name of the Committee of Public Safety, asked the Convention to take measures against female politicians. "Should women enjoy political rights and mix themselves up with the affairs of the Government? Universal opinion scouts the idea."[2] The Convention thereupon decreed the suppression of female clubs and societies, and subsequently prohibited any public assemblies of women. The female politicians completely disappeared.[3] They did not reappear until half a century later, in 1848. As a matter of fact, the agitation in favour of women's rights began soon after the Revolution of July, 1830. It was the socialist schools

[1] Lairtullier, "Les femmes célèbres de la Révolution" (P. 1840), t. ii., p. 180.

[2] "Moniteur," t. xviii., p. 299.

[3] Thus, says M. E. Legouvé in his book on "l'Histoire morale des femmes," ended almost without opposition this political rôle, in which there was no single act which can be called truly great. Women had, however, been giving admirable examples to France for four years, but it was by transient appearances as at the Federation festival or at the taking of the Bastille. . . Apart from these days of sublime intoxication, apart from these emotional actions which are the poetry of politics, but not politics itself, the interference of women was baleful, useless, or ridiculous (p. 407).

and the Saint Simonians in particular, which brought them to public notice.[1] The sympathies of the legislator were invited by petitions addressed to the Chamber by some women of action. The return of women to the political scene in 1848 was anything but successful. It needed all the firmness of conviction of Victor Considérant to propose to inscribe in the Constitution the political rights of women. The proposal, however, made on 13th June, 1848, in the Commission of the National Assembly, which was charged with elaborating a Constitution Bill, had no result.[2]

(3) Under the third Republic, the agitation in favour of Female Suffrage was resumed by persons of both sexes. After vain petitions to the Chamber and the Congress, they thought to claim the vote as a legal right. The question was subsequently brought before the tribunals, and finally, the Court of Cassation gave judgment as to the pretended political rights claimed for women. The administrative authorities had already had to deal with the question before it came before the tribunals. In 1880, when the electoral lists were under revision, certain women in Paris presented themselves at the *mairies*, and asked to be registered. When the municipalities refused to register them, the ladies in question retorted by declining to pay taxes, "leaving to men, who arrogate to themselves the right to govern, to make laws and draw up the budget, the privilege of paying those taxes which they vote and impose as they choose." The *Conseil de Préfecture* threw out that plea by laying

[1] See at the end of this volume Appendix I.: The Saint Simonians and Woman's Rôle.

[2] Garnier Pagès, "Histoire de la Révolution de 1848" (P. 1872), t. x., p. 366.

down in its judgment that the obligation to pay taxes was in no way correlative to the enjoyment or the exercise of political rights; that the law of April 21st, 1832, had determined that taxes had to be paid by every French inhabitant, and by every foreigner of both sexes, enjoying his rights and not reputed indigent; and that the words "enjoying his rights," were only used in a special and restricted sense.[1]

In 1885, when the *mairies* again refused to include women in the electoral lists, the women appealed to their local justices of the peace. The appeal was rejected. One of the claimants took her case to the Court of Cassation, basing her claim upon the comprehensive nature of universal suffrage, declaring that Frenchwomen were included as well as Frenchmen in the word *Français,* in accordance with the time-honoured Latin formula, *pronunciatio sermonis in sexu masculino ad utrumque sexum plerumque porrigitur* (a reference in speech to the male sex is generally applied to both sexes). Moreover, it was argued that the Constitution of 1848, the election decree of the same year, and the Government proviso of March 8th, 1848, had given so ample a meaning to the term "universal suffrage," that it could not be intended to exclude women from it, when its exercise had even been conferred upon freed slaves. The Court, in disposing of the appeal, delivered the following judgment:—"Whereas in accordance with the terms of Article 7 of the Civil Code, the exercise of civil rights is independent of the qualification of citizen, which alone confers the exercise of political rights, and is only acquired in conformity with constitu-

[1] "Droits des femmes," *Monthly Review* (1880), p. 151.

tional law; whereas, if women enjoy civil rights in the mode determined by law, according to whether they are married or single, no constitutional or legal provision confers upon them the enjoyment, and consequently the exercise, of political rights; whereas the enjoyment of these rights is a condition essential for enrolment on the electoral lists; whereas the Constitution of November 4th, 1848, in substituting universal for partial suffrage, from which women were excluded, only intended to confer on citizens of the male sex, who hitherto had been alone invested with such right, the right of electing representatives of the country to the several elective offices established by the Constitutions and the statutes; and this manifestly results, not only from the text of the Constitution of 1848, and the Acts of March 11th, 1849; February 2nd, 1852; July 7th, 1874; and April 5th, 1884, but still more from the spirit of these laws, attested by the labours and discussions which led to their being framed, and also by their application, uninterrupted and uncontested since the institution of universal suffrage, and the first formation, or revision in accordance with the new franchise, of the electoral lists; whence it follows that in declaring that Mde. L. B. ought not to be enrolled upon the electoral lists, the judgment impugned, so far from violating the provisions of the law referred to by the appellant, has made right and proper application thereof; the Court rejects, etc., etc."[1]

While approving of the decision of the Court as being in perfect accordance with the law, I cannot accept as satisfactory the grounds given by the High Court in its

[1] Judgment of the 5th March, 1885, in the Barberousse case.

judgment. The Court's first argument against the appellant's claims points out that no statute, constitutional or legal, has ever conferred political rights upon women. But the question is precisely whether a law is or is not needed to prevent women from having a vote. The lady appellant urged that as no law formally excluded them from voting, women were entitled to vote. The Court simply traversed the argument by stating that, as no law formally allowed them to vote, women were prevented from voting—one affirmation against another affirmation. The comparison made by the Court between the exercise by women of civil rights and the enjoyment of political rights (*i.e.*, "if women enjoy civil rights within the limits prescribed by law, no constitutional or legal provision confers upon them, etc."), while far from adding force to its argument, rather proves its deficiency and the strength of the contrary assertion. Indeed, whilst the Court contends against the political rights of women on the ground of the absence of express regulations regarding them, it brings forward on the other hand the presence in the Code of provisions regarding the civil rights enjoyed by women. But in reality, it is not by virtue of direct rules that women enjoy civil rights ; the law does not mark them out specially for this privilege any more than for the enjoyment of political rights. The Civil Code only makes special reference to the cases of incapacity of women as exceptions to the rule. So that whenever the law does not state the contrary, woman is reputed capable (even if Art. 8, which states that "every *Français* shall enjoy civil rights," did not in its extension apply to her). If the same system of interpretation were good with regard to the enjoyment of political rights, as the Court's comparison would lead one to believe, it would follow that, in the absence of restrictive measures regarding female political rights, women should be reputed legally capable to enjoy these to the full.

The second argument of the Court of Cassation is to the effect that the Constitution of 1848 intended the law of universal suffrage to apply to male voters only, "as manifestly shown" not only in the legal text, but even more in its spirit. In reality the legal texts do not "manifestly show" this at all. The decree of March 5th, 1848, about universal suffrage, and the subsequent texts which reproduced its provisions on the subject, do not expressly exclude women any more than they expressly include men. The term used for voters is usually "all French people (*tout Français*) of the age of 21 years." If this expression, which, according to the lady appellant, "includes both sexes," means, in the opinion of the Court, only persons of the male sex, it would be again begging the question, and the more so that in the civil law, which the Court had quoted in support of its argument, the expression, "*tout Français*," is admittedly applicable to both sexes.

There still remains the argument that the spirit of the electoral legislation and its practice are contrary to the admission of women to political suffrage. As a fact this is true enough, but, by itself, it cannot count as a reason. Might not one set against this the silence of texts upon the point, and avail oneself of the adage, "Expressa nocent, non expressa non nocent" (what is expressed injures; what is not expressed does not hurt). And if this rule, of such just application in every case where the rights of individuals in society are concerned, ought to give way to a higher principle, what is the higher principle upon which the judgment of the Court might take its stand?

(4) This principle of law exists, but it will not be brought to light so long as the old precept: "In dubio puto *materiæ subjecti et qualitati negotii* inserviendum et tribuendum *magis quam verborum formulæ*," which enjoins that greater stress should be laid upon the essence of the subject, and the kind of the matter, than upon the wording of the formulas, is disregarded. This rule, which is the very soul of juridical interpretation, is especially so in the domain of political law, for public law only formulates the great categories of a people's thought in what relates to the State; it often proceeds on broad generalisations latent in the national conscience.

The birth of liberty in the modern world has produced a double effect upon the relations of the individual to the State. It has guaranteed to man the enjoyment of his personal rights, of his individual liberty in all its manifestations, and, at the same time, it has called upon the citizen to participate in the government of the State. The rights that the new *régime*, vulgarly called constitutional, has undertaken to safe-guard are, in their very nature, inseparable from the personality of the man, being indispensable to the full development of his material and moral forces. The free enjoyment of these individual rights, whether of a public or a private character, should only be limited by that of other individuals. Participation in the government of the country is wholly different. Pre-supposing conditions of capacity, and not being indispensable to the development of the personality, it is not an absolute but rather a relative right. While the rights of the first category are, so to speak, pre-existent to the law which only intervenes to regulate their exercise, the other is a right conferred by the law. Consequently, whenever the question of the enjoyment of a political right is raised, it is to be decided, for the rights of the first kind, according to whether there is a law limiting such right, and, for the rights of the second kind, according to whether there is a law conferring such right. This is, in my opinion, what should be the fundamental rule of interpretation of public law.

Applied to electoral capacity, this rule, which I have found, furnishes us with a further rule, *viz.*, that the enjoyment and the exercise of the suffrage belong only to those expressly named by the law. Women, not being expressly named in electoral legislation, which speaks of *Français*, not of *Françaises*, of *citoyens*, not of *citoyennes*, are *eo ipso* debarred from the electoral franchise. And as the term *tout Français*, which is held to include both sexes in civil law, does not lend itself to such a construction in political law, woman cannot be admitted here except by a formal provision, established either by the written law or by the unwritten law, which is custom. In fact, positive law has refrained from doing so, and as for custom it always has been, and still is, adverse to the admission of women to political power; their exclusion from it was, as expressed by the orator of the Constituante, one of the principles "pre-existent in the mind of all French people." Consequently from the point of view of the political law in force for the time being, women's claims for enrolment on the electoral lists, in accordance with the law of the 30th November, 1875, or to be allowed to stand as candidates under the law of 17th July, 1889,[1] are inadmissible.

§ 2.—England.

(1) Admitted in England, as elsewhere, to feudal tenures, with the exercise of the rights of jurisdiction attached thereto, women were primarily, perhaps, not excluded from voting for members of the House of Commons. The evidence on this point is not very clear.[2] Certain documents relating to parliamentary elections of the fifteenth and sixteenth centuries seem to show that

[1] The law of July 17, 1889, which prohibits standing for Parliament for more than one constituency, binds the candidate to sign a declaration as to the particular division which he intends to contest, and if he does not perform it, in accordance with the provisions of that law, he is not allowed to post bills, or send circulars to the electors, or receive votes at the poll, etc.

[2] See "Modern Reports," or select cases adjudged in the Courts of King's Bench, Chancery, Common Pleas and Exchequers, 5th edit., corrected by T. Leach (London, 1796), vol. vii. Ingram *v.* Olive.

"The Law Reports," Court of Common Pleas (London, 1869), vol. iv. Chorlton *v.* Lings.

Chisholm Anstey, "On some supposed Constitutional Restraints upon the Parliamentary Franchise" (London, 1867). Report to the Social Science National Association, Department of Jurisprudence; Session of 10th June, 1867.

Chisholm Anstey, "Notes upon the Representation of the People's Act, 1867" (London, 1868), pp. 74-104.

Helen Blackburn, "Relation of the Women to the State in Past and Present."—*National Review* (London, 1886), v. 8.

women took part in the elections, especially in the manor towns. Aylesbury furnishes an example of this where, under Elizabeth, in 1572, the sole elector being a minor, his mother, Dorothy Pakington, lady of the manor, returned two members to Parliament. In 1628, there were produced before an election committee, parliamentary returns relating to the borough of Gatton, which contained the name of a woman. In 1739, in the King's Bench Court, when the question was under discussion as to whether a woman could be elected to the office of Sexton,[1] some more cases were cited, though from indirect sources. The Chief Justice mentioned that in a manuscript collection by the famous Hackewell, he found a case (Catherin *v.* Surry) in which it was expressly decided that a single woman *(feme sole)*, if she has a freehold, may vote for members of Parliament, but that, if married, her husband must vote for her.[2] On the other hand, the evidence of Coke[3] would tend to show that the exclusion of women from the suffrage was common law, as here:—

"In many cases, multitudes are bound by Acts of Parliament, which are not parties to the elections of knights, citizens, or burgesses; as all they that have no freehold, or have freehold in antient demesne, and *all women* having freehold or no freehold."[4]

"I do not know," said the Chief Justice, in 1739, "that it has ever been determined that women had not a right of voting. And whether they have not anciently

[1] Ingram *v.* Olive.

[2] "Modern Reports," p. 264.

[3] Sir Edward Coke (1557-1633), the great oracle of English jurisprudence.

[4] Institutes, iv., p. 5.

voted for members of Parliament, either by themselves or by attorney, is a great doubt."[1] But the Court unanimously decided that women had no longer the right to vote, if they had ever possessed it, because, as one judge expressed it, "the choice of members of Parliament requires an improved understanding, which women are not supposed to have."[2]

However, the British Empire was not entirely governed by Parliament. Considerable portions of its colonial domain were administered by large companies, the East India Company being among the best known of these. Organised on a commercial basis, on the shareholder system, the sole qualification necessary to have a voice therein, was to have vested interests. So female shareholders voted for members of the East India Council, which, till 1857, governed that immense Empire.

(2) When England, feeling the rebound of the French Revolution, received with marked favour the new gospel of liberty, preached on the banks of the Seine, the problem of the emancipation of woman was submitted to the judgment of British opinion. While William Godwin in his "Political Justice," developed the ideas of Rousseau to their very utmost, his wife, Mary Wollstonecraft, with unparalleled vigour, claimed the political emancipation of her sex in her famous book, "Vindication of the Rights of Women."[3] In popular societies, formed upon the model of those in Paris, women took a leading place; and not to be behind French revolutionary clubs, even

[1] "Modern Reports," 267.

[2] *Ibid*, p. 265. Opinion of Justice Probyn.

[3] London, 1792, 2nd edit., with a dedication "to M. Talleyrand Perigord, formerly Bishop of Autun." The work has lately been reprinted with an introduction by Mrs. Fawcett (London, 1890).

in terminology, English democrats coined the word "citizeness" as an equivalent for *citoyenne*. The violent re-action against "French Ideas," which ensued, put a stop to all democratic aspirations. But the "French Ideas" were not destroyed; Pitt could do nothing against them. Just as these ideas were leavening English society to the final triumph of the cause of democracy in general, so, too, minds continued to be stirred with regard to the social condition of woman. In popular movements, in the secret organisations which abounded in England after 1815, women played an important part. Academic Radicalism in its turn lent its support to the cause of women as early as in 1825.[1] But it was only when John Stuart Mill appeared to destroy so many of the old conceptions prevalent in English society, that the question of the emancipation of women had assumed in England real importance. In all his writings, he combated on woman's behalf what he considered to be antiquated prejudices and injustice, and he was not long in making converts. The entry of Mill into Parliament was the signal for political action in favour of female suffrage. Numerous petitions, signed by English ladies, were addressed to the House of Commons. And when, in 1867, Parliament dealt with the second Reform Bill, which proposed to extend the electoral franchise in boroughs to every man who was a householder rated to the poor rate, or a lodger resident for one year and paying a rent of £10, Mill brought forward an amendment substituting the word *person* for the word *man*. The House received Mill's proposal with all the deference due to so

[1] Cf. "The Appeal of Women," by W. Thompson and Mrs. Wheeler (London, 1825).

great a thinker, but rejected it by 196 votes against 83.

(3) The Reform Bill of 1867 was voted without women being allowed to benefit by its provisions, and the champions of women's rights were going to resume their agitation, when certain lawyers discovered that, legally, women were already entitled to the electoral franchise. This was their argument. In former centuries women had enjoyed the right to vote; no legislative enactment had taken it away; thus they were in full possession of their electoral capacity. The first Reform Bill of 1832, it is true, expressly stated that the new franchise was granted to every "male person who," etc. But, firstly, this restriction related only to the franchises introduced by that act, and not to the old electoral qualifications,[1] as, for instance, that of forty shilling free-holders. Again, the Act of 1867, establishing a new franchise, no longer used the term "male person," but "every man." And as statute 13 and 14 Vict. c. 21, s. 4, commonly called Lord Brougham's Act, provided that "in all Acts, words importing the masculine gender shall be deemed and taken to include females, unless the contrary be expressly provided," the term, "every man," in the Bill of 1867 should be held applicable to either sex, as there is no "express provision to the contrary." Moreover, besides Lord Brougham's Bill, the word man

[1] The Act of 1832, as well as subsequent electoral Reform Bills, did not completely supersede the former legislation; each new Bill extended the franchise to a new class of electors, so that after 1832, as after 1867 and 1884, there was not a single qualification for the electorate, but several qualifications of different origins, placed side by side with one another.

and its equivalent *homo* are in good English and Latin generic, and include men and women. The great maxim, "omnes homines equales sunt" (all men are equal), embraces entire humanity. In the law of England the word *man* is used in the same sense, particularly where political rights are concerned, in Statutes which relate to the Constitution of the realm, so early as the Magna Charta which has "Nullus liber homo capiatur vel imprisonetur . . . nec super *eum* ibimus, nec super *eum* mittemus. . . ."[1] (No free man shall be arrested nor imprisoned. . . . We shall not go for *him*, nor send for *him*. . . .)

This argument seemed so irresistible to the advocates of Female Suffrage that they abandoned agitation, and women decided to tender their votes at the next election. An incident which occurred in the interim at Manchester served to confirm them in this resolution. By an oversight the name of a woman was inscribed on the voting list, her Christian name resembling that of a man. As no one noticed this, her name remained on the list. At the bye-election which took place at Manchester in 1867, this lady presented herself at the poll, and her vote was accepted. To partisans of Female Suffrage, this seemed a fact of great importance; "it carried Female Suffrage from the region of possibility to that of practical politics, and thus gave the movement a powerful impetus."[2] In a con-

[1] See Chisholm Anstey's papers cited above, and also a brief review of the argument by Dr. R. Pankhurst, "The Right of Women to vote under the Reform Act, 1867," *Fortnightly Review*, September, 1868.

[2] "First Annual Report of the Executive Committee of the

siderable number of towns, women, having the property qualification of electors, claimed to be put on the register.[1] Though this was refused in some places, in others it was granted. In several parishes the overseers, not knowing if women had or had not a vote, put their names on the register merely in order that the question of their right to vote might go before the Court of Registration. The Revising Barristers, who had to deal with the appeals against the admission or non-admission of women, were by no means agreed as to the application of the law. Most of them rejected the claims of women, struck out the names registered by the overseers, and in one instance (at Leeds), the Revising Barrister fined the applicant for making "a frivolous claim." But in some Registration Courts, women were more successful. The Revising Barristers recognised their right to vote ; some by virtue of Lord Brougham's Act, others by virtue of the old law, admitting the *feme sole* ; others, again, because in doubtful cases it was right to interpret the law in favour

Manchester National Society for Woman's Suffrage" (Manchester, 1868), p. 5.

[1] The electoral register in England is made out by the parish overseers of the poor, who keep the lists of those rated to the poor rate, which serves as a basis for the register. Appeals against the overseer's decision are taken to the Registration Court of the district, held every year, for the revision of the lists, by a member of the Bar, called a Revising Barrister, who is appointed for each county and borough within the circuit by the Senior Judge of Assize, and in London by the Chief Justice. As a general rule the Revising Barrister corrects material errors that are brought to his notice, but introduces no changes in the lists, unless the parties make a claim that a name should be inserted, or an objection against the retention of a name admitted by the overseers.

of the extension of the franchise, or because it was not their business to ascertain whether the votes of women were legally good or not, their duty being confined to retaining on the register all names against which there was no objection. About two hundred and thirty women were finally registered. But the matter did not end here.

(4) At Manchester, which became the centre of agitation for Woman's Suffrage, more than 5000 women had appealed against the decisions of the Revising Barristers. All these appeals were dealt with collectively, in a test case.[1] The grounds of appeal raised before the Court by the counsel who argued in favour of Woman Suffrage (and who is at the present moment Lord Chief Justice of England) contained the arguments we have mentioned above, that is to say, (1) that in past times there was no distinction of sex in regard to electoral qualification, and that it had not been introduced by subsequent legislation; (2) that the Act of 1867, if interpreted in conformity with Lord Brougham's Act, gave the suffrage to women, even if it did not belong to them before; and (3) that the use of the word *man* in the Act of 1867 in place of the words *male persons* in the Act of 1832 conferred it in express terms.

The Chief Justice, in giving judgment, was of opinion that if women formerly took part in parliamentary elections, the historical precedents quoted were of comparatively little weight, as opposed to uninterrupted usage to the contrary for several centuries; and what has been commonly received and acquiesced in as the law, raises a strong presumption of what the law is; that therefore

[1] Chorlton *v.* Lings, L. R , v. iv., 1869.

the argument drawn from the alleged fact that no law had annulled the women's right to vote was ineffective; that the Act of 1832, which confined the franchise in boroughs to *male persons*, had, on the contrary, sanctioned the exclusion of women, and that there could be no doubt that at the time of the passing of the Act of 1867, the common understanding of both lawyers and laymen was that women were incapacitated from voting, and that the legislator must be presumed to have acted under the same impression. If there was no doubt that, in many statutes "men" may be properly held to include women, in others it would be ridiculous to suppose that the word was used in any other sense than as designating the male sex. Nor could the more extended sense be given to the word *man* in the present case by Lord Brougham's Act; Section 56 of the Act of 1867 providing that the franchises conferred by it were in addition to, and not in substitution of any existing franchises, and Section 59 of the same Act stating that it shall be construed as one with the enactments for the time being, it follows that the words *male persons*, of the Act of 1832, referred to electors in general without any distinction as to their qualification. If the legislator of 1867 wished to introduce so important an alteration as the extension of franchise to women, it is difficult to believe that he would have done it by using the word *man*. He has, therefore, said the Chief Justice in conclusion, used the word *man* in the same sense as *male persons* in the former Act; that this word was intentionally used in order to designate expressly the male sex; and that it amounted to an express provision, in conformity with Lord Brougham's Act, that every man as distinguished from women, possessing the qualification, was to have the franchise. Upon both grounds, therefore—first, that women were legally incapacitated from voting for members of Parliament, and, secondly, that the provisions of the Act of 1867 were limited to men and did not extend to women—the Chief Justice thought that women were not entitled to the franchise, and that the decisions of the Revising Barristers must be affirmed. The other judges concurred with his Lordship's opinion, being careful to point out that the exclusion of women from the suffrage was not on account of their intellectual inferiority, but from a desire to promote decorum, and in this way it was rather a privilege and a homage paid to the sex—*honestatis privilegium,* as the great Selden remarked.[1]

After this appeal, based on the erroneous application of the Act of 1867, another case relative to Woman's Suffrage was brought before the Court.[2] The female applicant claimed her right to vote in virtue of a statute of the fifteenth century—8 Henr., VI., c. 7—which conferred such right upon forty shilling freeholders. The Court dismissed the claim, declaring that its judgment in the previous case of Chorlton *v.* Lings did not only apply to the particular question of elections for boroughs, but embraced the whole question of the right of females to vote in the election of members of Parliament.

The point of law once settled, the Court decided that the appeals of women against the decisions of the Revising Barristers were inadmissible. In the case of Wilson *v.* Town Clerk of Salford, the Court ad-

[1] Opinion of Justice Willes (L. R., 388).
[2] Chorlton *v.* Kessler, *ibid*, 388.

mitted the defendant's argument, that the appellant, in her position as a woman, had no *locus standi*, and found that "only males were *persons* within the meaning of 6 Vict., c. 18,[1] and had a right to appeal under the provisions of that Act, and that the Court had therefore no authority to hear this case." [2]

The judgment of the Court of Common Pleas being final, the question of Woman Suffrage was judicially settled. Beaten in the Law Courts, the partisans of political rights of women turned again to the legislator.

The proposal made in Parliament in 1870 for granting Woman Suffrage was again rejected. Similar attempts have been made many times since, but without success. Subsequently, women have obtained a vote at local elections, but as to votes at parliamentary elections, they are still agitating for it. Such disparity became an additional argument for the political emancipation of women.[3] They

[1] That is the Registration Act of 1843, Section 42 of which enacts that *every person* who has made a claim to be entered on the list, or whose name has been erased . . . shall have the right of appeal. . . .

[2] L. R., iv., p. 399.

[3] In a memorial presented to the Prime Minister in 1873, they observed (1) that a property qualification being the basis of representation throughout the kingdom, both for Imperial government and for local government, it was an anomaly and an injustice, that where property belonged to a woman, the franchise which was attached to it should be inefficacious as regards Imperial government, whereas for local government women were not similarly incapacitated ; (2) that the Imperial franchise was more important to women than the local franchise, not only because the burden of Imperial taxation was heavier than that of local rates, but also because in local government the two sexes were treated on an equal footing, as ratepayers, and not as men and women, whilst the Imperial Parliament passed

demand that their rank as ratepayers be recognised, with all its political consequences, that women who are paying taxes, which give men the right to vote, be equally entitled to enjoy that right. At the passing of the last electoral Reform in 1884 (which extended to the rural population the franchise conferred on inhabitants of boroughs by the Act of 1867), the occasion seemed to many friends of Woman's Suffrage specially propitious for getting Female Suffrage on the Statute-Book. The

different laws for men and women, and the latter obtained less than justice in several departments of legal and social order ; (3) that if you followed the effects produced by legislative extension of the franchise to new social *strata*, you could not fail to remark that the middle and lower classes had been more frequently consulted and had seen their interests more carefully looked after since they had obtained the franchise, and that the same result would certainly follow as regards women if they were admitted to the franchise ; (4) that the legal inequalities, of which women were the victims, were greater and more palpable than those to which any other class of the nation was subject before they obtained political power. In fact, women had to complain of insufficient means of education, restrictions on the liberty which they ought to possess of taking up honourable and lucrative professions, difficulty of obtaining a livelihood, a want of security in the enjoyment of their property and income, and when they were married the loss of the right of guardianship of their children, which was a denial of a mother's rights, etc. These grievances* and several others, which were the direct result of the legislation in force, were so many examples of the position of inferiority in which women were kept by the law. The sole guarantee of good government for men, and it was equally so for women, was to consult the governed on the choice of governors and the making of laws ("Sixth Annual Report of the Executive Committee of the Manchester National Society for Women's Suffrage, 1873," p. 10, etc.).

* On some of these points women have already obtained what they wanted.

number of its partisans in Parliament had greatly increased since the beginning of the agitation; nearly every new division in the House showed numerical progress, especially in the ranks of the Liberal party. In 1884 this party was in power. But Mr. Gladstone considered that an amendment in favour of women, introduced into the Bill for the extension of the Franchise, might imperil its success, and intimated to his party that it would be better not to raise the Women's Rights question. A zealous minority, however, broke through the chief's orders, but met with defeat. Since then, the bulk of the Tory party sided with the cause of Women's Rights. Disraeli was from the first in favour of allowing women to vote. During the discussion of the last Reform Bill in the House of Lords, Lord Carnarvon, one of the most eminent Tory statesmen, said that when they were going to enfranchise two millions of men, some of them confessedly ignorant and illiterate, he could not see on what principle of justice they could exclude a small section of persons who, by intelligence, by the possession of property, and in every conceivable quality of fitness, were called to exercise the right of voting, and would exercise it fairly and well. Women took part in local elections. Why, then, should they not take part in parliamentary elections?[1]

The conversion of the Tory party considerably increased the chance of women's admission to the Parliamentary Suffrage. But still the hour of their enfranchisement is not likely to come so soon as many of its too sanguine

[1] Hansard's "Parliamentary Debates," 3rd series, vol. ccxc., p. 381.

supporters expected. The last parliamentary debate upon Woman Suffrage, in 1892, showed that there is yet in the House of Commons a powerful majority, made up of members of all parties, who are most decidedly opposed to increasing the electorate by giving women a vote.

While they have not yet attained the goal of their ambition in Great Britain, the champions of women's political emancipation have had the satisfaction of seeing their hopes realised (in 1881) in a small corner of the great British Empire—in the Isle of Man.[1] By virtue of a law, proclaimed, according to ancient custom, from the top of Tynwald, on January 31st, 1881, female owners of real estates valued at an annual rental of £4 were admitted as voters for the *House of Keys.* For persons of the male sex, the electoral franchise is more extended; besides proprietors, occupiers and lodgers are allowed to vote. The House of Keys was for conferring this right upon

[1] The Isle of Man, situated in the Irish Sea, near the south-west coast of Scotland, with an area of 227 square miles, and a population of 54,000 persons of Celtic race and language, has kept up its old institutions from the time it had kings of its own. England is there represented by a governor appointed by the Queen. The Manx people govern themselves through the *Tynwald Court*, which consists of two chambers. The Upper Chamber or *Council*, presided over by the governor, is composed of the principal dignitaries of the island, civil and ecclesiastic, to the number of nine. The other chamber, or *House of Keys*, consists of twenty-four members elected by the citizens who have the property qualification (proprietors, householders, and lodgers). The laws voted by the Tynwald Court are sanctioned by the Queen, acting apart from the English Parliament, or, to use the old constitutional phraseology, by the *Queen in Council*, not by the *Queen in Parliament.*

women of all three categories, but in a dispute upon this question with the other chamber it was worsted.[1]

In the Colonies several attempts have been made to secure Woman's Suffrage. The proposal was more than once brought before the Legislatures of Canada, South Australia, Victoria, New South Wales, and New Zealand,[2] but without success.

§ 3.—The United States.

(1) The spirit of implacable austerity which animated the men who went forth to the New World to seek for liberty and to found an empire was anything but favourable to the admission of women to public life. The Bible, which the Pilgrim Fathers knew by heart, declared that in congregations woman should be silent. The examples cited to prove that in the colonial period women voted, are extremely rare and inconclusive. In the colonial charters and constitutions electors are styled "persons," "freeholders," "freemen," and "inhabitants," without stating their sex;[3] but, practically, the distinction was observed. Since the Revolution the new State Constitutions, drawn up with greater legal precision, introduced the definition "male," as in the case of the Massachusetts Constitu-

[1] On the details of this dispute we may refer to an article published in the *Englishwoman's Review*, 1881, p. 20.

[2] According to the latest intelligence (September, 1893) from Australia, the Legislature of New Zealand passed an Electoral Reform Bill which confers the right of franchise upon women.

[3] Except in Virginia, where it was enacted that "no woman, sole or covert," even though a freeholder, should have a voice in the election of burgesses (1Will. III., c. 2; 3 Geo. IV., c. 2). See Mr. Cortlandt F. Bishop's elaborate "History of Elections in the American Colonies," N. Y., 1893, p. 65.

tion of 1780.[1] To see in this fact evidence that up to that time women used to vote (for if women had not the suffrage before, would they have thought it necessary to insert that clause?[2]), seems to me more ingenious than convincing. There is only one certain precedent of the admission of women as voters; it is that of New Jersey. The Constitution of 1776 gave the suffrage to all the inhabitants who had the property qualification. A law

[1] In doing so the framers of the Constitution have simply interpreted public opinion as it manifested itself very clearly during the discussion by the people of Massachusetts of the scheme of the Constitution. So, at a Convention held for this purpose at Ipswich, in the county of Essex, the delegates, who were well versed in the current theories on natural rights, and were not ignorant of the writings "of a learned foreigner named Rousseau, a citizen of Geneva," expressed themselves as follows:—"In every free State the person of every member and all the property in it ought to be represented, because they are objects of legislation. All the members of the State are qualified to make the election, unless they have not sufficient discretion, or are so situated as to have no wills of their own. Persons not 21 years of age are deemed in the former class from their want of years and experience. . . . . . Women, whatever age they are of, are also considered as not having a sufficient acquired discretion, not from a deficiency in their mental powers, but from the natural tenderness and delicacy of their minds, their retired mode of life, and various domestic duties. These concurring prevent that promiscuous intercourse with the world which is necessary to qualify them for electors" (Essex result of the convention of delegates holden at Ipswich, in the county of Essex, to take into consideration the Constitution and Form of Government proposed by the Convention of the State of Massachusetts. *Bay. Newbury Port*, 1778, reprinted in the "Memoirs of Theoph. Parsons, Chief Justice of Mass.," Boston, 1859, p. 376).

[2] C. B. Waite, "Who were Voters in the Early History of this Country?" (*Chicago Law Times*, 1888, October).

passed 22nd February, 1797, to regulate elections under that Constitution, provided in Article 9 that every voter shall deposit his or *her* ballot, and that the written ticket shall contain the names of those for whom he or *she* votes.[1] But a later Act of 1807 enacted "that no person should be allowed to vote except free-born white citizens of the male sex." Since then the word *male* has been inscribed in the Constitution of the State of New Jersey, as had already been done in the other States.

It was only about the middle of this century that the movement in favour of Female Suffrage was started in the United States. Mary Wollstonecraft's vindication of the rights of her sex, indeed, have reached America, and her arguments have been brought before the public at meetings and lectures; but it was by another road that the natural-right theory came to support the cause of women's political emancipation. It was the abolitionist movement which paved the way for Women's Rights. Claiming for the negro the rights inherent in human nature, the abolitionists insisted on the complete equality of mankind, which rejects every distinction, especially if based upon physical qualities. If white men had not the monopoly of liberty, if blacks too had an equal right, could women be shut out from this? Their claims seemed the more admissible that when the agitation against slavery began, women threw themselves into it with all the ardour of their nature.

Soon the demand for Female Suffrage became more general. Initiated by a few persons of very independent manners—which "society" found rather too indepen-

[1] Paterson's "Laws of New Jersey," 1800, p. 230.

dent—the crusade for Women's Rights soon rallied many eminent men, and among them Lloyd Garrison, Wendel Phillips, Frederick Douglas, Charles Sumner, and other famous abolitionists. In 1848, the women held their first convention at Seneca Falls (New York). A "declaration of sentiments"[1] was drawn up, claiming for women political equality, as a right proclaimed in the Declaration of Independence by the fathers of the Republic. These had, in fact, stated as "self-evident truths that all men were created equal, that they were endowed by their Creator with certain unalienable rights, and that among these were life, liberty, and the pursuit of happiness; and that, to secure these rights, governments were instituted among men, deriving their just powers from the consent of the governed."

When after the Civil War the negroes obtained their liberty and therewith the right to vote, women demanded with fresh energy that they too should be allowed to enjoy a similar privilege. Since then Congress has repeatedly had to deal with proposals to extend the franchise to women through federal legislation. As the legislator did not make haste to alter the Constitution for them, women endeavoured to take part at elections under the existing laws. Then the question of Female Suffrage was brought before the tribunals, and even submitted to the Supreme Court of the United States, just as it had been in England and in France But at the outset, in imitation of the example of illustrious ancestors, certain women sought to resist male

[1] The text of the *Declaration* is given in the "History of Woman Suffrage," edit. by E. C. Stanton, S. B. Anthony, and M. J. Gage, N.Y., 1881, vol. I., pp. 70-71.

tyranny by refusing to pay taxes so long as their right of representation was not recognised. In several States this method was adopted before the War of Secession as well as after 1865; but, of course, without success.[1]

(2). Under Grant's presidency the question of women's right to vote was referred to the Courts in the following circumstances. The Constitutions of all the States reserved the franchise expressly for "male citizens." But that did not conclude the question in the opinion of the partisans of Female Suffrage; they claimed that the provisions of the several Constitutions should be considered null and void; for they were contrary to the Constitution of the United States, Amendment XIV. of which[2] prohibited the States from passing laws which

[1] Some of those who protested allowed the tax collectors to distrain their goods year after year. The account of one of these cases is related for the edification of the public in a book entitled "Abby Smith and her Cows, with a Report of the Law Case decided contrary to Law," by Miss Julia E. Smith. Hartford, Conn., 1887. It is the story of a lady farmer of Connecticut, who refused to pay her taxes, and whose cows were distrained one after the other. The book is ornamented with a wood engraving of the cows in question.

[2] The supplementary provisions of the Constitution of the Union are codified in the form of additional articles called amendments. The following is the text of Sec. 1 of Amendment XIV. "All persons born or naturalised in the United States, and subject to the jurisdiction thereof, are citizens of the United States, and of the State wherein they reside. No State shall make or enforce any law which shall abridge the privileges or immunities of citizens of the United States; nor shall any State deprive any person whatsoever of life, liberty, or property without due process of law; nor deny to any person within its jurisdiction the equal protection of the laws." This amendment was adopted in 1868 in order to secure to the recently enfranchised negroes the indisputable enjoyment of their civic rights.

restricted the privileges and immunities of citizens, and the right of suffrage was one of these privileges. The Courts had therefore to decide on the constitutional legality of the provisions excluding women from the suffrage.

Washington, the capital of the Union, had the first judicial discussion of the question. The Act organising the district of Columbia,[1] of 21st February, 1871, placed women in exactly the same position that the Constitutions of the States gave them; it also reserved the franchise for "male citizens." The Supreme Court of the district had to examine appeals preferred against decisions refusing women enrolment on the electoral lists and admission to the ballot. The Appellant's counsel, with a vast array of learning reaching from Aristotle to Savigny and Chisholm Anstey, unfolded the argument that the franchise was, under the American system, a natural right; that, by virtue of the old English *common law*, which was the source of American rights and liberties, women enjoyed the suffrage, and the amendments to the Constitution of the United States prohibited any abridgement of this privilege. The Court dismissed the appeal. In its judgment it took particular care to disallow the plea of natural right. Pointing to the constitutional history of the Republic, the Court laid down that the right of suffrage, however varied might be the conditions imposed by the laws of different States for its exercise, invariably depended on the express authority of the political power,

[1] As is well known, there has been detached for the seat of the Government of the United States a small belt of land, which is not a part of any State whatsoever; this district, where the city of Washington has been built, is placed, under the name of Columbia District, under the exclusive jurisdiction of Congress.

and was exercised within the limits assigned by positive law.

"Passing from this brief allusion to the political history of the question to the consideration of its inherent merits, we do not hesitate to believe that the legal vindication of the natural right of all citizens to vote, would, at this stage of popular intelligence, involve the destruction of civil government. There is nothing in the history of the past that teaches otherwise. There is little in current history that promises a better result. The right of all men to vote is as fully recognised in the population of our large centres and cities as can well be done, short of an absolute declaration that all men shall vote, irrespective of qualifications.

"The result in these centres is political profligacy and violence verging upon anarchy. The influences working out this result are apparent in the utter neglect of all agencies to conserve the virtue, integrity, and wisdom of government, and the appropriation of all agencies calculated to demoralize and debase the integrity of the elector. Institutions of learning, calculated to bring men up to their highest state of political citizenship, and indispensable to the qualifications of the mind and morals of the responsible voter, are postponed to the agency of the dramshop and gambling hell; and men of conscience and capacity are discarded, to the promotion of vagabonds to power.

"This condition demonstrates that the right to vote ought not to be, and is not, an absolute right. The fact that the practical working of the assumed right would be destructive of civilization is decisive that the right does not exist."

As to the meaning of Amendment XIV., which provides that all who are born or naturalised in the United States and subject to their jurisdiction, are *citizens*, the Court admits that women are clearly *citizens* in so far as *citizens* are opposed to foreigners, and that every citizen is capable of being invested with the right of suffrage, but that that can only be done by the authority of the legislative power. As this power, in Columbia District, has not conferred the suffrage on women, they cannot be considered as possessing it.[1]

Some time after, at the presidential elections of 1872, a certain number of women presented themselves at the poll in the State of New York, again under cover of Amendment XIV. Their claim was admitted, and they gave their votes for the President and Vice-President of the Union, and for the representatives of the State at Congress. Thereupon the federal authorities intervened. All the women who had voted, to the number of 14, were put in prison, along with the "inspectors of election," who had received their votes. The Bill against these women was thrown out, except as regards one, Suzanne Anthony, who for many years had been the leading spirit of the agitation for Woman Suffrage. This lady and the "inspectors of election" were committed to the Assizes of the Federal Court (District Court of the United States of America in and for the northern district of New York) on the charge of an offence provided for in Section 19 of the Federal Law of

[1] "Women Suffrage in the Supreme Court of the District of Columbia," in general term, October, 1871. Sarah J. Spencer *v.* The Board of Registration, and Sarah E. Webster *v.* The Judges of Election. Reported by J. O. Clephane. Washington (Judd & Detweller), 1871, pp. 68-72.

30th May, 1870—the lady for "having knowingly voted without having the legal right to vote," and the others for "having deliberately and wilfully accepted votes of persons who had not the electoral franchise." Suzanne Anthony was found guilty and sentenced to a fine. The inspectors of election suffered the same fate.[1]

(3) In 1874, the question of the right of women to vote was brought before the Supreme Court of the United States, the great tribunal of the Union in matters pertaining to constitutional law. Dealing with an appeal presented by a lady of the Missouri State, the Supreme Court came to the conclusion that the expression, "citizens of the United States," conveyed the idea of membership of a nation and nothing else; that it applied to women as much before the adoption of Amendment XIV., as since; that the qualification of citizen in no way implied the enjoyment of electoral rights; that the Union had no electors of its own creation; that its electoral body was only composed of electors in the States; that suffrage was not co-extensive with the citizenship of the States, either at the time of the formation of the Constitution of the United States, or since the adoption of Amendment XIV.; that this amendment did not add to the privileges and immunities of a citizen; that it

[1] The arguments set forth in the pleadings and in the Court's address to the jury do not add anything to the question of the constitutional right in dispute. I need not recapitulate them, but will content myself with referring to an account of the case published in the volume, "An Account of the Proceedings on the Trial of Susan B. Anthony on the Charge of Illegal Voting at the Presidential Election in November, 1872, and on the Trial of the Inspectors of Election by whom her Vote was Received." Rochester, N. Y., 1874.

simply furnished an additional guarantee for the protection of such as he already had; that the suffrage not being one of the civic privileges and immunities over which a State has no control, a provision in a State Constitution which confines the right of voting to "male citizens of the United States" was no violation of the Federal Constitution, and that in all States where this provision existed, *women had not the right to vote.*[1]

The conclusions of the Supreme Court of the United States did not differ much from the arguments used in the judgment of the Columbia District Court. But the judgment of the Federal Court alone had the *auctoritas vis:* it decided the question for the whole Union.[2] The point of law was thus irrevocably decided, and the petitioners had to fall back upon the legislator.

(4) They found a welcome reception in certain "Territories" only. Territories are those parts of the Union not yet formed into States, being as yet only in an embryo condition. When virgin lands, reclaimed in the desert of the Far West or from the Red Skins by adventurers, pioneers, have attracted a certain population within

[1] Case of Minor *v.* Happersett. See "Cases Argued and Adjudged in the Supreme Court of the United States." Reported by John W. Wallace. Washington, 1875. Vol. xxi., pp. 162-178.

[2] The judgment of the High Court has not, however, carried conviction to all minds, even to those of the higher representatives of public authority. So the Governor of Massachusetts, in his message to the State Legislature in 1882, expressed himself on Women's Suffrage in the following terms—"For myself I believe that that right is given them by the Constitution of the United States. By the decisions of the Courts I am overruled in my action on this subject, but not in my convictions." ("Appleton's Annual Cyclopædia," 1882, p. 516.)

fixed settlements, and the rudiments of civilised life have more or less taken root, the federal authority acknowledges the political individuality of these agglomerations. The Territory over which these settlements are dispersed, generally very large, is then officially organised by an Act of Congress. A government modelled on that of the States, but with more limited powers, is established. The Governor and the chief officers are appointed by the President of the United States. The laws passed by the Legislature of the Territory may be annulled by Congress. The delegates from the Territory to Congress have only a right to speak without voting. In a word, the Territories are minor members of the great political family of the United States, When the economic and political development of the Territories show that they have attained their majority, Congress admits them to an equal share in the Union; they are promoted to the rank of States.

An Act of Congress of 1868 carved out in the "great American desert" the Territory of Wyoming, which then consisted of about 5000 souls gathered in a few towns along the Union Pacific Railway. The first session of the first Legislature of Wyoming was not at an end when a proposal was made to give the suffrage to all women who had completed eighteen years. It was treated as a joke, and the amendments proposed to the Bill were each more ridiculous than the other; one legislator wished to insert the words "all coloured women and squaws; another preferred for women to read *ladies;* a third suggested to alter the limit of age from 18 to 30, and explained that, if this amendment was carried, Woman Suffrage would remain a dead letter. The Bill was carried amidst laughter by both Houses, and finally received the approval of the Governor on 12th December, 1869.

According to one of the former Governors of Wyoming, the vote would have been lost but for a piece of sharp practice of a shrewd member of the Legislature.[1] But it

[1] This is the version of the ex-Governor, John W. Hoyt. His account is as follows :—"People smiled generally. There was not much expectation that anything of that sort would be done ; but this was a shrewd fellow who managed the party card in such a way as to get, as he believed, enough votes to carry the measure before it was brought to the test. . . ." Thus he said to the Democrats : — "We have a Republican Governor and a Democratic Assembly. If we join in making the Assembly adopt the Bill, and if the Governor vetoes it, we shall have made a point, you know ; we shall have shown our liberality and lost nothing. But keep still ; don't say anything about it." The Democrats promised. He then went to the Republicans, and told them "that the Democrats were going to support his measure, and that if *they* did not want to lose capital they had better vote for it too. He did not think there would be enough of them to carry it ; but the vote would be on record, and thus defeat the game of the other party." And they likewise agreed to vote for it. So when the Bill came to a vote it went right through. The members looked at each other in astonishment, for they had not intended to do it *quite*. Then they laughed and said it was a good joke ; but they had "got the Governor in a fix." So the Bill went, in the course of time, to John A. Campbell, who was then Governor—the first Governor of the Territory of Wyoming—and he promptly signed it. His heart was right. He saw that it was a long-deferred justice, and so signed as gladly as Abraham Lincoln wrote *his* name to the "Proclamation of the Emancipation of Slaves." ("Address upon Women's Suffrage in Wyoming," delivered at Philadelphia by Governor John W. Hoyt. London, 1882, p. 4).

Cf. "The Working of Woman Suffrage in Wyoming," by Mr. Horace Plunkett, *Fortnightly Review*, May, 1890, pointing out the inaccuracy of the above account.

seems that his colleagues were quite willing to be deceived; that they have adopted Woman Suffrage for the sake of advertising the new Territory which wanted to attract emigrants and capital. Directly the Governor had affixed his signature to the Bill, the news was telegraphed in all directions, and the Territory, the name of which was hardly known, suddenly acquired the wished-for notoriety. It was in fact there that the right of suffrage was for the first time granted to women. The law in question, entitled, "An Act to Grant to the Women of Wyoming Territory the Right of Suffrage and to hold Office," found a place in the code of Wyoming under chapter 50 in the following terms: "Every woman of the age of 21 years, residing in this Territory, may, at every election to be holden under the laws thereof, cast her vote. And her rights to the elective franchise and to hold office, shall be the same under the election laws of the Territory as those of electors."[1]

The Second Legislature voted the repeal of the Act, but the Governor of the Territory vetoed the repeal. In the statement of reasons, which he was obliged to furnish, he insisted at length on the right of women to take part in the government of their country, and on the excellent results which had followed the exercise of the suffrage by the women of Wyoming. As at the new discussion rendered necessary by the veto, the Bill annulling the Act of 1869 did not receive in one of the Houses the required two-thirds majority, the veto retained its full effect, and Female Suffrage remained in force.

[1] The Compiled Laws of Wyoming (1876), p. 348.

In 1890, the Territory of Wyoming was admitted as a State. In making its demand, it had, in accordance with established rule, to submit, for the preliminary approval of the voters, a draft of the future Constitution of the State, drawn up in a convention specially selected for that purpose by the people. The Constitution sanctioned Woman Suffrage, and being submitted *en bloc* for ratification by the people, was accepted. The United States Congress made no objection to the clause relating to Woman Suffrage, admitted the Territory into the Union, and thereby acknowledged that the exercise of a political vote by women was not incompatible with the Constitution of the United States.

(5) Soon after the adoption of Woman Suffrage in Wyoming, it was introduced into the neighbouring Territory of Utah, which is well-known to fame in connection with the Mormon sect, which, so to speak, altogether created the country. In order to maintain their dominant position there against the immigrant *gentiles*, the *Saints* got an Act passed in the local legislature to admit all women to the suffrage. This law, which came into force on 12th February, 1870, provided "that every woman, of the age of 21 years, who has resided in this Territory for six months next preceding any general or special election, born or naturalised in the United States, or who is the wife, widow, or the daughter of a native, born or naturalised citizen of the United States, shall be entitled to vote at any election in this Territory."[1] In a polygamous community, the electoral powers of women

[1] The Compiled Laws of the Territory of Utah, 1876, Salt Lake City, p. 88 (title iii., chap ii., sec. 43).

could not but be considerable, and, in fact, this has served to keep up polygamy in Utah.[1] So the Federal authority, which engaged in a struggle against Mormonism, attacked Female Suffrage. By a first Act of 22nd March, 1882, passed by virtue of its powers over the Territories, Congress decided that no polygamist or bigamist, or any woman co-habiting with such, could take part in any election whatever, or be elected in any Territory or in any other place under the jurisdiction of the United States.[2] The wives of monogamists and unmarried women were not affected by this Act; they kept their vote where it had been given them by the local law.

But a new federal law of 19th February, 1887, withdrew the suffrage from all women in Utah, without exception. Section 20 of the Act, called the Edmunds-Tucker Bill, provides "That it shall not be lawful for any female to vote at any election hereafter held in the Territory of Utah for any public purpose whatever, and no such vote shall be received or accounted in any manner whatever; and any and every Act of the Legislative Assembly of the Territory of Utah, providing for or allowing the registration or voting by females is hereby annulled."[3]

(6) Lastly, a third Territory introduced Woman Suffrage, the Territory of Washington, which forms the extreme limit of the United States possessions in the North-West, between the State of Oregon on the south and the Dominion of Canada on the north. Woman

[1] Compare the speech of Senator Beck of Kentucky, at the sitting of the Senate of the United States, on the 14th December, 1882.

[2] Revised Statutes of the United States, sec. 5252.

[3] United States Statutes, 79th Congress, chap. 397, s. 20.

Suffrage was there adopted by a law of 22nd November, 1883, and confirmed in 1886 by the law on electoral registration, which spoke of the electors *of the male or female sex,* and provided that the term *he* was always to be understood as *he or she.* But after it had been in force for three years and a half, the Supreme Court of the Territory declared the Act of 1883 null and void, because it was not in conformity with the rule, which required that the contents of each Act should be stated in the title at the head of the text; and the Act of 1883 was entitled, *An Act to Amend Sec.* 3050, ch. 238 of the code . . . , whereas to be valid it ought to have borne the title, *An Act to Confer the Electoral Franchise on Women.*[1] The legislators of the Territory set to work to pass another Act, giving women the vote (law of 18th January, 1888), and this time adding a proper heading. But the Court declared the new law null and void, because the Territory had no right to confer the suffrage on women. The Act of Congress of 23rd March, 1853, which organised the Territory, did not, in the opinion of the Court, include women among "the citizens of the United States," of whom the electoral body of the Territory ought to consist, for in respect to the exercise of the suffrage, men only were at this time held to be citizens.

If we refer to the Act organising the Territory,

[1] The question was brought before the Court in consequence of an appeal presented by a convict in the Assize Court. He based his appeal on the presence of women on the jury, where, according to the law, only electors could sit. The appellant's argument was that women did not possess this qualification, because the Act of 1883, which claimed to give it them, was null and void as not fulfilling the technical conditions of the law.

we find that Congress contented itself with laying down the following provisions on the subject of the electorate: The qualification necessary to be an elector and to be elected shall be such as shall be determined by the Legislative Assembly, provided that the right shall be given only to citizens of the United States above 21 years of age, etc. The condition of sex not having been reserved in this Act, and the term *citizens of the United States* merely signifying subjects of the United States,[1] did the Legislature of the Territory of Washington exceed its jurisdiction in passing a law to give women a vote? That is the real question. They certainly did *not* exceed their jurisdiction. The interpretation of the texts, and still more, the attitude of Congress in reference to the right of Territorial Legislatures to confer on or withdraw from women the political suffrage, point to this conclusion. When the Legislature of Wyoming was pleased in 1869 to confer the vote on women, Congress did not decide that it had violated the Act organising the Territory, which determined the electoral qualification for Wyoming, in the same terms as were employed in the Act organising the Territory of Washington. Congress indeed excluded the women of Utah from the suffrage, but they did so by virtue of the discretionary powers, which they exercise over the Territories, not because they disputed the constitutional right of the Utah Legislature to confer such a privilege. In the same way Congress could summarily have annulled the laws of 1883, 1886, and 1888 in the Territory of Washington, but they did not

[1] As was decided by the Supreme Court of the United States in the case of Minor *v.* Happersett.

do so, as they did not think fit, in those particular cases, to make use of their powers.[1] At the present time, the question with regard to the Territory of Washington, which since 1889 became a State, has only a retrospective interest. When on the eve of its admission into the Union, the draft of its Constitution was submitted to the voters of the Territory, they rejected the provisions concerning Female Suffrage.

At the present time, the only part of the American Union where women are admitted to political suffrage, is the new State of Wyoming, which is only a little spot on the immense political surface of the United States. For though it fills an area equal to that of Italy or the half of France, it has not even a hundred thousand inhabitants. In other States the agitation for the extension of the suffrage to women continues in two directions; one party is for gaining this end by means of a federal law like that which, under the form of Amendment XV. of the United States Constitution, imposed upon all States the admission of negroes to political rights; the partisans of Women's Rights claim in their favour a sixteenth Amendment. In a parallel direction to the national agitation, an agitation is also carried on to obtain Female Suffrage from the local Legislatures in each respective State. This double campaign has not yet come to anything. More than once the question has been dealt with in Congress, and women have been allowed to set forth their claims in committee. The senators and the members of the House of Representatives have one and all listened to them with the greatest courtesy,

[1] Compare "Suffrage in Washington Territory," by W. S. Bush. *Chicago Law Times*, vol. iii., Jan., 1889.

without, however, being brought to their way of thinking. With the Legislatures of the States, women have been more successful, and have succeeded in getting their vote in more than one State.[1] But the consent of the two Houses and the sanction of the Governor are not sufficient, as in the Territories, to give the force of law to a new constitutional measure; it must have the ratification of the people, and the people invariably throw out bills conferring Female Suffrage.

§ 4.—An Indirect Suffrage.

Now that we have examined the legislation and the jurisprudence of the countries where women have, or thought that they have, political suffrage equally with men,[2] it remains to see if women are admissible to share in the electoral franchise in any indirect ways.

(1) The first country which gives an answer to such inquiry is Austria. The legislative power is there divided between the Imperial Parliament, or *Reichsrath*, and the local Diets. All the legislative powers not reserved

[1] Colorado, Oregon, Nebraska, Indiana, South Dakota. The plebiscite in this last State, which took place at the end of 1890, admitted to the franchise the "civilised" Redskins, but rejected the clause relating to Woman Suffrage. The figures of the ballot are not wanting in interest: there voted against Woman Suffrage, 45,682 electors, for Woman Suffrage, 22,972; against the suffrage of the Indians, 29,593, for the suffrage of the Indians, 38,676 (*The Woman's Journal*, Boston, 27th December, 1890).

[2] In Holland, in consequence of a claim made by a woman to be enrolled upon the electoral lists, the High Court of the kingdom (Hoog Raad) decided in 1883, that female voting was contrary to the intentions and the fundamental principles of the Constitution. In the revised Constitution of 1887, the word *male* was accordingly entered in all the provisions relating to elections.

to the *Reichsrath* are left to the Diets of the kingdoms and principalities of which Cisleithania is composed. These local assemblies, as well as the *Reichsrath*, legislate with the sanction of the Emperor. *Reichsrath* and Diets emanate all from the same electoral body; it is the electors of the Diets who choose the members of the House of Representatives of the *Reichsrath*. Re-established with some scraps of ancient local liberties, or created anew by the Letters Patent of 1860, the Diets were a sort of compromise between the ancient feudal traditions and the modern spirit of equality. They were organised on the antique model with hereditary nobles, bishops, and commons. In the first place large landowners were given a special representation in those assemblies. Similar recognition was granted to other interests; they were divided into three special electoral groups—rural communes, chambers of commerce and trade, and towns. In this last group, besides ratepayers, there were also included persons possessing an educational qualification, as university graduates, schoolmasters, etc. Thus the modern principle of personality as the basis of the electorate was introduced. But, on the other hand, the organisation of the first electoral group was founded upon the old-fashioned conceptions which considered property as the principal source of all rights, whilst almost ignoring the personality of its possessor. So the enjoyment of the electoral right was recognised in the class of large landed proprietors, as belonging to all its representatives, whoever they were, corporations as well as individuals, military men in active service, in some countries minors as well as persons of age, and especially women as well as men. But if, in granting them the right of the franchise, the legislator chose to ignore their personality, he could not do this when it came to the exercise of the suffrage. These *electors* created by him being incapable, or reckoned incapable, of exercising their right by themselves, the law decided that it should be exercised in their name by other persons: that of corporations by individuals, that of minors by majors, that of military men by civilians, that of women by men. Thus the rule was established that, in the large landholder class, women should enjoy electoral rights, but that such rights should be exercised by deputies whom they might choose for that purpose. Introduced into one of the compartments of the Austrian constitutional edifice by a reminiscence of the feudal past, woman has since benefited by the modern spirit, and has been admitted in some parts of the monarchy even to the plebeian electoral groups, *viz.*, those of towns and rural communes.

We will now examine in detail the legal provisions regulating the right of women to a political vote in the several parts of Cisleithania.

(2) The electoral statute for the *Reichsrath* thus determines the electorate: "In general, the electoral right shall belong to every Austrian citizen of the male sex who is in enjoyment of all his rights, and has completed his twenty-fourth year. Only in the electoral class of the large landed proprietors, or of the highest taxpayers,[1] women, if they are in their own right, and are twenty-four years of age, are considered to possess the right of voting" (§ 9 of the law of April 2nd, 1873).

[1] In Dalmatia the first electoral group is composed of those who are highest taxed.

According to § 12, "Everyone having the right of voting exercises this personally, as a general rule, but in the class of large landed proprietors, or of the highest taxpayers, suffrage can be exercised by proxy." After stating that military men in active service and corporations shall exercise by proxy the electoral right attached to their property, the law of the empire lays down that "women are to exercise their vote in this class (the landed proprietor class) in the manner prescribed for its exercise at Diet Elections" (§ 14).

The provisions upon that subject, contained in the Election Regulations of the several Diets, are not identical, nor are they drawn up with the same distinctness of expression. But still it is evident from them that women in the large landed proprietor class everywhere possess electoral capacity.[1] The ordinance for Bohemia declares that "women . . . . may exercise their electoral right in the class of large landed proprietors only by proxies designated by themselves" (§ 10 of the Law of January 9th, 1873). The proxy for this purpose can only be given to an elector of the same class (§ 11), who is thus to add to his own vote that of the woman. For the "kingdom of Galicia and Lodomeria, with the grand Duchy of Cracow," the law of Sept. 20th, 1866, lays down that in the case of women living with their husbands, the husband shall exercise the electoral right; other women who are *sui juris*[2] give their votes by proxies.

1 Except in Vorarlberg, where the class of large landed proprietors does not exist.

2 This qualification somewhat limits the electoral right of women in Galicia; for Article 1 of the same law grants this right

The Electoral Statute of Moravia contains the same provisions, with this notable difference that the right of women to the suffrage is not limited to the large landed proprietor class. Paragraph 16 of the Electoral Statute states in general terms: "Persons not *sui juris* exercise the electoral right through their legal representatives, married women through their husbands, and other women *sui juris* through proxies."

The electorate of the electoral groups of towns and rural communes being composed not only of ratepayers but also of persons qualified on account of the educational standard, as I have already stated, it became a question in Moravia if women, admitted to the vote in these two classes, enjoyed such right by virtue of educational qualifications. In rural communes, for instance, the right of vote was granted without any rate-paying condition to the head masters of public schools appointed by decree, "alle mit Decret angestellte Lehrer der-Volks- und Bürger-Schulen." Was such a privilege to be shared by female teachers? The Supreme Court (Reichsgericht) decided that the electoral capacity could not be held to extend as a matter of right to female teachers, who were consequently excluded from the suffrage.[1]

Similar regulations, with regard to the rights of women to vote in all the electoral groups (large landed proprietors, towns and rural communes), are to be found

to large landed proprietors who are not *sui juris*, by allowing them to use it through their legal representatives or proxies appointed by their representatives, whilst as regards the electoral right of women the law stipulates that they must be *sui juris* (eigenberechtigt).

[1] Judgment of the Court, Oct. 13, 1884 ("Sammlung der Erkentnisse des Reichsgerichts,") by Dr. A. Hye von Gluneck, t. vii., No. 304.

in terms more or less explicit in the laws of Salzburg,[1] Silesia,[2] Tyrol,[3] and Vorarlberg.[4]

(3) The statutes of Carinthia and Krain on the other hand expressly provide that in the town and rural commune groups men alone possess the suffrage.[5] The statutes of the two first countries cited, those of Bohemia and Galicia, are silent with regard to women in the popular electoral groups. The laws of Bukowina, Dalmatia, Göritz with Gradiska and Istria, Styria and Upper Austria abstain from any mention of female voters. Nor has the statute of Lower Austria any provision for the admission or the exclusion of women. The absence of any mention of them in the text of the laws seemed to give rise to doubt. If there was no doubt concerning women of the large landed proprietor class, to whom the suffrage is given by the electoral law of the Empire, uncertainty still prevailed as regards the groups of towns and rural communes. In these two classes all municipal voters are electors for the Diets, and women have a municipal vote in all the rural communes.[6] Does it not then follow that in all these places women have a right to vote for the Diets, even in the absence of any more explicit provision? To dispel these doubts,[7] a recent law of Lower Austria, of

[1] Landtagswahlordnung, § 15.

[2] Law of 22nd November, 1875, § 16.

[3] Landtagswahlordnung, § 15.

[4] Landtagswahlordnung, § 9.

[5] Landtagswahlordnung für Kaernthen, § 12, 14; Landtagswahlordnung für Krain, § 10.

[6] Further on I shall treat these questions in detail.

[7] Compare the speech of Deputy Dr. Haberl at the sitting of the Diet of Lower Austria, on 3rd January, 1891.

June 3rd, 1889, stipulated that the suffrage for the Diet belonged to persons of the male sex except in the class of large landed proprietors, where women *sui juris* were held to possess electoral powers.

In brief, for Diet Elections women have the right to vote, by proxy, in the electoral colleges of the large landed proprietors in the whole of Austria, and, also, in the colleges of towns and rural communes in several Cisleithanian countries, whilst for the Reichsrath Elections this right only belongs to women as large landed proprietors.

As regards eligibility, women are expressly excluded from the Reichsrath (§ 19 of the Law of April 2nd, 1873), and implicitly from the Diets.

(4) An indirect suffrage is likewise granted to women in Sweden. The Houses of the Swedish Parliament (Riksdag) are both elective. One, the popular House, has as its electoral basis the whole population, every inhabitant having an equal vote (one man one vote), if he possesses the property qualification to become a member of the electoral college; and only individuals of the male sex in full enjoyment of their rights may be voters for the Lower House. The Upper House, which represents the "interests," is not elected by the direct votes of the electors, but by the organs of local self-government, that is, by the provincial assemblies (landstings) and the municipal councillors of great towns, who in their turn are chosen by municipal colleges, formed not on the basis of the number of electors but upon that of their contributions to public expenditure, the vote of the higher-taxed counting more than that of the lower-taxed. As here personality gives place to

property, all property owners enjoy the electoral right, corporations as well as individuals, minors as well as majors, and finally, women as well as men. In elections of persons chosen to elect the Upper House, women may only vote at the first stage. Their direct intervention does not extend beyond the municipal suffrage, but, thanks to the peculiar Constitution of the Second Chamber, their vote is re-echoed, so that members of the Upper House are indirectly elected by women at third hand in the case of rural communes, and at second hand in the case of towns.[1]

§ 5.—Delegation and Attribution of the Property Qualification.

If a woman cannot vote in person, or by a male proxy, can she transfer to another the property qualification in countries where the franchise depends on it?

(1) In France, at the time of the establishment of the property franchise under the Restoration, the question was settled in the affirmative, but within very narrow limits; a widow might make a transfer of her qualification to a male member of her family in order to constitute or complete his franchise. The choice of the person to be delegated was at first extremely limited. The law of June 29th, 1820, directed that the property taxes paid by a widow might be reckoned

[1] In the following chapter, devoted to local self-government, I shall have occasion to refer to the Swedish municipal organisation. It is sufficient to mention here that the municipal electors vote for the *landstings* directly in the towns and at second hand in the rural communes.

to the son; in default of sons, to the grandson; and in default of grandsons, to the son-in-law whom she should appoint. The electoral power thus conferred on women by the law was very small. The law of April 19th, 1831, considerably extended it. The ninth Article of this enactment added grandsons-in-law to the number of relatives who could be invested with the property qualification for the vote, and granted the widow full liberty of choice among sons, grandsons, sons-in-law, and grandsons-in-law, so that she could name a son-in-law even if she had sons. Moreover, this benefit was extended to divorced and even partially divorced women (Art. 8). The law-courts interpreted these provisions in a broad sense. Thus it was established that a widow could communicate her property qualification to the following persons, *viz.:* to an adopted son, a son-in-law whose wife had died without issue, or a son-in-law who, after the daughter's decease, had contracted a second marriage, provided that there existed issue of the former marriage.[1]

At the present time Italy is the only country where women have the right to transfer the property qualification entitling to the franchise. By virtue of Art. 12 of the electoral law of September 24th, 1882, "the direct taxes paid by a widow or a woman legally separated from her husband may be reckoned to one of her sons, grandsons, or great-grandsons appointed by her."[2]

There was also a similar provision in the law of Luxembourg. The ordinance for the elections to the

[1] See the judgments cited by Dalloz, *Répertoire*, Droit politique, § 279.

[2] "Annuaire de législ. comp.," xii., p. 511.

State assemblies of June 7th, 1857, contained the following in its seventh Article :—" A widow can have her taxes reckoned to that son, or in default of sons, to that son-in-law living under her roof, whom she may appoint."[1] But the electoral law of May 28th, 1879, in reference to elections to the Chamber of Deputies, has repealed this clause.[2] M. Eyschen, Minister of State in the Grand Duchy, in the learned treatise which he has recently published on the public law of Luxembourg, points out that such a clause was not admissible as regards elections to the Legislature, because the fifty-second Article of the Constitution required the elector himself to pay the taxes which conferred the franchise.[3] However, this Art. 52 was copied from Art. 53 of the revised Constitution of November 27th, 1856, and the latter did not prevent the passing of the law of 1857, which granted to widows the right of transferring their property qualifications.

(2) The indirect influence on the elections which women possess, or possessed, by virtue of their right to transfer their property qualification, only belongs to women *sui juris,* and does not extend to married women. The contributions paid by the latter are imputed, in some countries where the franchise depends on a property qualification, to their husbands, in order to make up their qualification. That is to say, the taxes paid by the wife are reckoned to the husband as a matter of course by virtue of his marital power. Already the delegation

1 "Pasynomie Luxembourgeoise," 1855-1858. Luxembourg.

2 Compare Art. 8 of this law (in the "Lois et règlements sur l'organisation politique, judiciaire et administrative du Grand-Duché de Luxembourg," collected by P. Ruppert, Luxembourg, 2nd ed., 1885.)

3 "Das Staatsrecht des Grossherzogthums Luxembourg," Freiburg, 1890 (Marquardsen's collection), p. 155.

of property qualification in the cases I have mentioned is bordering upon private law and recalls the women's tutelage of olden times. When women were under perpetual guardianship, a widow's guardian was usually her own son. The electoral law, by conferring on a widow paying taxes the right to choose a proxy from her sons, or, in their default, from her sons-in-law, did not give her, so to speak, more than a choice between a certain number of possible guardians. When we come to the legal provisions by which the wife's taxes are imputed to the husband, we reach the extreme limit of the domain which we have proposed to explore, and which is that of public law, and we begin to trespass on that of civil law. "This is a kind of homage paid to the power of the chief of the family, which society does well to surround with the greatest authority," said Lainé, in the French Chamber of Deputies, on January 5th, 1817, when that matter was under discussion of the House.[1]

In England and Scotland, where, according to the old common law, "the wife was merged in the husband," the latter had the advantage of his wife's real property as a qualification for the Register. But the Married Women's Property Act of 1882, which assimilates the married woman to the *feme sole* as regards her power over her property and income, has had the effect of limiting the husband to his personal property for the purpose of constituting or completing his qualification.[2] In the United States the question has followed the same course. Till 1888, there was still, amidst the triumphant democracy of America, a State, that of Rhode

[1] "Moniteur" of 6th January, 1817.

[2] Rogers on Elections, Lond. 1885, 14th edit., vol. i., p. 8.

Island, which required of the elector the possession of real property. The condition in which women were placed by the English common law had been already considerably modified in 1844. In 1872, a fresh law decided that "the real property of a married woman should be *absolutely* secured to her sole and separate use." Inevitably the electoral status of the husband was changed by this. On the initiative of the Governor, the Supreme Court of the State acknowledged this (in 1878) by deciding that the husband could no longer vote in virtue of his wife's property, unless he had married her before 1872, and she had acquired her property previous to that date; but that if the marriage had been contracted after the promulgation of the new law, or if the woman's property had been acquired since 1872, the husband could not claim on such property his right to vote, unless children capable of inheriting that property had been born of the marriage.[1] Thus it was no longer *jure mariti* that he voted, but as father of the children.

In France, under the property franchise *régime*, the law of February 5th, 1817 (when Lainé made the remark quoted above), caused the husband to profit by the taxes paid by his wife, even if she was partially divorced from him. The proposal to except the case of such a separation was rejected in 1817, on the ground that while deciding on the separation of husband and wife, the judges only pronounced on household matters and for family peace, but that the husband's legal qualification was in no degree modified. The law of April 19th, 1831, abandoned this system, and

[1] Appleton's "Annual Cyclopædia" (1878), p. 732.

reckoned to the husband the taxes of his wife, whether with separate or joint property, only so long as there was no partial divorce between them (Art. 6).

It is under similar conditions that taxes of the wife are reckoned to the husband in Belgium, Luxembourg, Italy, Prussia and Roumania.[1] Article 3 of the Dutch electoral law (of 4th July, 1850) containing a similar proviso was repealed in 1887. The same result was achieved in Spain by the introduction in 1890 of universal suffrage as had happened before in France when the property qualification for electors was abolished. Thus the right of husbands to vote by virtue of their wives' property ceases, since they no longer need it.

To recapitulate the facts set forth in this chapter, we find that all women of full age are admitted to vote in the State of Wyoming; that in the Isle of Man the suffrage is granted to female owners of real estates; that unmarried women belonging to the great landed proprietor class may vote by proxy for the Austrian Reichsrath, as well as for the Local Diets of the Cisleithanian countries; that in some countries of the Austrian monarchy the same right is granted to women of the other electoral classes; that in Sweden women share indirectly in the formation of the Upper House; and that in Italy widows and women partially divorced from their husbands may have their taxes transferred to a member of their family in order to constitute or to complete his qualifications for the franchise.

[1] Article 12 of the Belgian Electoral Code modified by the law of 22nd August, 1885 ("Annuaire de législ. comp.," xv. 371); Art. 8 of the Luxembourg Law of 28th May, 1879; Art. 8 of the Italian Electoral Law of 1882; the Prussian Electoral Laws (viv. infra); Art. 14 of the Roumanian Electoral Law of 8-20th June, 1884. ("Annuaire," xiv., 682).

CHAPTER III.

Local Self-Government.

§ 1.—General Observations.

(1) The notion of *self-government,* of which England has given to other countries both the experience and the name, which is now a part of general political language, is applied specially to local self-government, as administered by representatives of the people and not by agents of a central bureaucracy. Local self-government deals primarily with local economic interests, and it is only in a secondary degree that it includes powers of a political character. These last being too complex to be treated successfully by the State alone, are partly delegated in all free countries to the agency of local self-government. Its organs are therefore, in character and competence, partly public and partly private.

The primitive type of self-government—the village community of the Middle Ages—had its origin, its basis, and its *raison d'être* in the administration of common property. It was a natural, a spontaneous association devoid of any political character. With all the autonomy which it succeeded in acquiring, it partook so little of political liberty that it was able to exist under the most different systems of government, not excepting the most despotic. We find it in India to-day with the same character as in Europe in the Middle Ages. Conquerors succeeded conquerors on the banks of the Ganges; the rural commune retained its autonomy unchallenged.[1] Again in Europe it existed side by side with serfdom, and to-day exists under Russian autocracy. Collectivist at first, and still so in some places down to the present day,[2] the village community gradually allows the emergency of individual property, but on the other hand it preserves for general use undivided property, commons, the Germanic *allmenden.* Here in the common interests pertaining to forests, pasture land, wells, and village watch, the village community reasserts itself, is living a life of its own, and goes on thus for centuries. Not that it rises to the ideal of corporate personality; on the contrary, the villagers do not distinguish the commune from the individuals of which it is composed. It does not occur to them, therefore, that communal affairs can be decided except by one and all. In order that the community should do anything, every member must raise his arm; in order that it should move in this or that direction, every member must put his leg forward. Witness the repugnance that exists in Russian village assemblies of the present day to the decision of a mere majority.

[1] Compare G. L. Gomme, "Village Community." London, 1890.

[2] In Russia, to a certain extent, and even in Germany, in some backward districts. See on this subject R. Morier, "Systems of Land Tenures in Various Countries," and Sir H. Sumner Maine, "Village Communities," 3rd edit. London, 1876, p. 78.

"In the eyes of the *Moujik* everything in the *Mir* must be done unanimously. It is the consent and the common will of the members of the assembly that give it its authority. That a decision should be regarded as valid, as free from error or fear, in fact, obligatory on all, it must in this primitive democracy have the support, or, at least, the acknowledgment, of all the members."[1]

It was the same in the communities of the Middle Ages and in the village assemblies, particularly in France. They were attended by those who "would, should, and could," *touz ces qui hont voluy, dehu et pehu,* as an old communal charter of Burgundy, relating to a communal transaction in the year 1331, puts it. Women, widows, and spinsters were present in the same right as men. "Their consent," says M. Babeau, "added to the validity of the contract, which was not binding on those who were not mentioned in it."[2] Neither was there any age qualification. Everyone who had an interest had a place in the assembly. The very name by which the communal right was frequently described showed how comprehensive it was; it was called right of *vicinage,* and the members of the assembly were *les voisins* and *les voisines.*[3] An instrument relating to a lease in fee, concluded with the Abbot of

[1] Anatole Leroy-Beaulieu, "L' Empire des Tsars," P., 1881, II., p. 34. *Cf.* similar remarks (of earlier date) in Ashton Dilke's "Essays on Local Government," Cobden Club Series, London, 1875, p. 94.

[2] "Le village sous l'ancien régime," 2-e éd., P., 1879, p. 33.

[3] So especially in the Pyrenees, as in Bigorre, in Bearn ("De Lagrèze, La féodalité dans les Pyrénées"). P. 1864. *Cf.* the "neighbours," *vicini* of the title of "De migranticus" in the Salic Law.

Saint-Savin in 1316, sets out that the neighbours, male and female, of Canterets (*bésis et bésiés*), collectively and individually, being present and consenting, being neither deceived nor bribed, nor induced by artful promises, nor compelled by force, but of their own free will and pleasure, with full knowledge of the matter, have openly declared their unanimous approval, with the exception of Gaillardine de Frechon, *tots exceptat la dite Gailhardine del Frexo.*[1] In another instrument three centuries later (1612), relating to the communal Constitution adopted for a village in the canton of Scey-sur-Saône, we learn that it was drawn up in the presence of the notables of the place assembled, "under the elm, before the common hearth where the said inhabitants were accustomed to assemble for the business of their community," and that among these notables were present two women, a widow and a girl.[2] More records might be cited which mention the presence of women at the communal deliberations in different places. It is not easy to establish with certainty whether the participation of women in communal assemblies was of right or only exceptional. M. Babeau, who treats it as exceptional, admits that "it is difficult at certain periods to ascertain who was, and who was not, a member of the assemblies." [3]

(2) In France, as elsewhere, the triumph of absolute monarchy, with its overpowering centralisation, has destroyed the communal autonomy of the villages. The

[1] De Lagrèze, op. cit., p. 82.

[2] "Revue des sociétés savantes des départements, 5e série, t. I., anneé 1870." P. 1871, p. 510.

[3] Loc. cit.

strong levelling blast of the Revolution extinguished the little vitality which they had left. Rural communities were assimilated to urban communities in the sense that both became administrative subdivisions, cast in the same mould. At the same time, the levelling State was good enough to grant to the inhabitants of town and country the same political rights. These rights have cloaked, not to say submerged, the whole local public life. Although the rural community, in consequence of the occupations of its inhabitants, remained, to a great part, a centre of homogeneous concrete interests of a private character, the communal right, as such, was swallowed up in the political right; the members of the community were merged in the body politic; and as women form no part of the latter, they found themselves formally excluded from the communal right, even when the commune attended purely to the material interests of its members. Such were the effects of the Revolution on local self-government, and on the part played by women in it.

Once only there appears like a flash in the legislation of the Revolution a decree of the Convention which, in a special case, summons women to vote. This Assembly had, as we have already seen, very little tenderness for the rights of women. What is there, then, in this particular case? It deals with common property. The village community presents itself to the legislator's mind for a moment in its ancient conception, with its primitive *raison d'être*, and the legislator allows himself to be transported into the past, into the times of *voisins* and *voisines*, and for the special occasion he calls together men and women "collectively and individually," not as of old, "under the elm before the common hearth," but in the polling booth. The decree of 10th and 11th June, 1793, which charges the municipal authority to call together the inhabitants to deliberate on the partition, sale, lease, or enjoyment of common property, provides in its fifth article that at the "assemblies of inhabitants" called together for such purpose, "every individual of either sex, having the right to share in the common property, and of the age of 21 years, shall have the right to vote."

The establishment of universal suffrage, under the second Republic, deprived communal right of that frail economic basis which the property qualification had supplied. Women could no longer be admitted to the enjoyment of this right on the ground that they were municipal stockholders, for the stock company had been dissolved. Henceforward they could claim the vote on philosophic grounds only. Pierre Leroux undertook to do it for them at the Legislative Assembly. On the 21st November, 1851, during the discussion of the Communal Elections Bill, he proposed an amendment to the article which provided that "the list of electors shall consist of all Frenchmen of full age." The amendment of the St. Simonian philosopher substituted the words: "Frenchmen and Frenchwomen of full age,"[1] but it was not adopted.

(3) In the Germanic world, although the difference between the rural communities and the urban communes has not been entirely obliterated, yet there, too, the village communities have changed their character. The bonds of association, formed in the sphere and on

[1] "Moniteur" of the 22nd November, 1851.

the basis of common interests, were relaxed in proportion as the common property was divided, and the real servitudes interchanged between the communal proprietors, fell into disuse. As the economic basis of the ancient village community grew weaker, monarchical centralisation, more vexatious and more penetrating in its regulations than the feudal lords whom it supplanted, began in its turn to contribute to the decline of the rural community. In this process of disintegration of the ancient communal society, sometimes its concrete personal element, and sometimes its *real* element[1] comes prominently into view, but the two are no longer united in a living whole, but separate and isolated.

In South Germany, and in Switzerland, the communal right, *das Gemeindebürgerrecht* (the burgher right) comes to depend upon descent from burgher parents; it is transmitted from generation to generation like an inheritance; it is personal without being individual. At length the conception of "the man in himself" introduced by the French Revolution comes in here too to individualise communal as well as political rights. In the name of equality of rights a struggle is beginning between the burghers (Bürger), the domiciliaries (Einsæsse or Hintersæsse), and the residents (Aufenthalter), a struggle of which Switzerland has been and still is the special arena.

However, in the northern countries of the Germanic world, the communal right takes a midway position

[1] As a matter of fact intermediate shades were evolved in the course of the transformation of the Germanic communal right, but it is unnecessary for us to dilate on the topic here; I need only refer to the great work of O. Gierke, "Das Deutsche Genossenschaftstrecht," Berlin, 1868, I., p. 725, etc.

between the right detached from the soil and personal to an individual (of a particular category), and the right personal to the individual: it accepts as the qualification possession of real property, without regard to the person· Thus connection with a concrete group which has given such a character of exclusiveness to the corporate life of towns is no longer required; while, on the other hand, no recognition is accorded to the human atoms into which the political rationalism of the eighteenth century had dissolved modern society.

Property having in this way become the exclusive basis of the right, and the personality of the owner being henceforth completely disregarded, is not the difference between the sexes an idle distinction? In fact, we find that throughout nearly the whole Germanic world—the Germans, Anglo-Saxons, Scandinavians—where communal right has a real as opposed to a personal basis, woman is admitted to the enjoyment of it. Thus the feudal rule that the law of the soil overrides the law of the person reappears, but it is now applied in a wider and at the same time a narrower sense. Property in land having become democratised, there is no longer any distinction between noble proprietors and commoners. But on the other hand public right being no longer confused with private right, the admission that powers of a public character should be an appurtenance of property right ceases. Therefore, while granting the communal right to women (as well as to companies and corporations) by virtue of their property right, care has been taken to limit it to that sphere of local self-government which is devoid of all political character, and concerned chiefly with the administration of the economic interests of the place. The development of modern civilisation has produced its social effects principally in towns; the new wants it has created have multiplied and complicated public functions there to such an extent that when the powers delegated by the central authority are also taken into account, the self-government of cities assumes a character which makes it very much resemble the government of a State. The municipal suffrage acquires there a range that almost makes it a political franchise. Consequently the communal suffrage of women has generally been limited to country districts or to towns of minor importance. Where it has been confined to rural communes it encounters fewer obstacles, inasmuch as the difference between the sexes is there slighter in every respect.[1]

In certain countries the capitalist character of the present economic system has introduced, side by side with possession of realty, the payment of taxes as a condition for the exercise of the communal vote. By this arrangement women of course benefit equally with men wherever females are admitted at all to communal rights. But where the communal right no longer rests on a material basis that brings back the community to its origin and its economic *raison d'être*, women find themselves excluded from communal suffrage. Directly they have to claim it under circumstances which strip it of

[1] Compare W. Riehl, "Die Familie," Stuttgart, 1882, especially Chapter II., *Die Scheidung der Geschlechter im Processe des Culturlebens*, where the author shows how closely country women resemble men in respect of their occupations, manner of life, thoughts, costume, figure, voice, head, etc., and how in town life and generally in civilised society, the line of separation becomes more and more marked.

its non-political character, as, for example, under the system of universal suffrage, where it is confounded with the parliamentary franchise, they are absolutely non-suited.

Now that we have learned the origin and nature of the communal suffrage of woman, let us examine in detail the legislative provisions on the subject in the several countries.

§ 2—England.

(1) Local government in England is administered by a considerable number of diverse agencies without any system, and often without any connection one with another, as they work within areas which sometimes meet, sometimes part, and sometimes intermix with or intersect one another. "Local government in this country," says a writer, "may be fitly described as consisting of a chaos of areas, a chaos of authorities, and a chaos of rates."[1] Without undertaking the somewhat irksome task of dispelling this triple chaos, I will content myself with pointing out the territorial units and the elective offices to which are assigned the public functions of local government, in order to see what share of power is there allotted to women.

The primary unit of which all the organisations in local government both in town and country are made up is the (civil) parish. It is the old township, and it received its present name from the ecclesiastical unit which came to be grafted upon it, and which shares with it its administrative agencies whilst preserving

[1] M. D. Chalmers, "Local Government." Lond., 1883, p. 17.

its own character. The parish is the primary territorial unit for the assessment of the poor rates which, by itself, is the most important business of English self-government, and upon which several other assessments are modelled. All who pay poor rates on the land and houses which they occupy within the limits of the parish have a vote. Like the freemen in the days of the township, they meet at a general assembly, termed the *vestry*, to decide on their common affairs. The votes are reckoned in proportion to the amount of their rates, on the basis of one vote for every £50 of rateable value up to a maximum of six votes. In populous parishes the full assembly can delegate its powers to a council selected from its own members, termed a *select vestry.* To take part in a vestry meeting there is no condition of residence; payment of rates is all that is necessary. Personal ties count for nothing; property alone is taken into account, and all its representatives are allowed to vote, women as well as commercial companies. It ought, however, to be added that, at the present time, vestries have but scant powers, their functions having been gradually, in course of time, transferred to other bodies. The principal power — the relief of the poor — has been almost entirely transferred to the guardians of the poor, in consequence of the great reform of the Poor Laws in 1834. Since that time a number of other duties of local administration, which have nothing in common with the relief of the poor, have been repeatedly transferred to the guardians, so that the Union has become one of the most important, if not the most important, intermediate division between the parish and the county At the election of guardians women take part exactly as at parish vestries, for the guardians are chosen in each by the ratepayers.

One word as to the manner in which women vote. At the full meetings of the vestry they may attend in person, just as in the rural communities of the Middle Ages the *voisins* and *voisines* were present, *collectively and individually*. For the election of guardians, women, like male electors, vote at home. The police distribute voting-papers from house to house, and return a few days later to collect them.

(2) Side by side with the civil parish is still in existence the ecclesiastical parish. The administrative agency of the ecclesiastical parish is the vestry, in the primitive sense of the term, consisting of the clergyman, the churchwardens, who are *ex-officio* overseers of the poor, and parishioners. Every member of the parish, that is to say, every ratepayer, can take part in the meetings of the ecclesiastical vestry just as in those of the civil vestry. Women are not excluded. It is a common law right. But it is worthy of note that the written law does not favour the participation of women in parish affairs. Thus, so recent a law as the Public Worship Regulation Act of 1874 (which authorises parishioners to lodge with the bishop protests against the conduct of priests in regard to the observance of rites, the ceremonies, and the ornaments of the church),[1] provides that the term parishioner is to be taken to mean "a male person."[2]

[1] This Act was passed in consequence of the Ritualistic movement, which introduced into public worship within the Church of England ceremonies resembling those of the Roman Catholic ritual.

[2] 37 and 38 Vict., c. 85, sec. 6.

(3.) Whether women are eligible to parochial offices of an ecclesiastical character is a question on which the texts are silent. With regard to the office of sexton, we have the decision of the Court of King's Bench in 1739 in the famous suit of Ingram *v.* Olive (cited above), by which it was decided that a woman could be invested with these duties. As to the office of churchwarden, it appears that women are equally eligible to it, the only qualification required being that of *inhabitant householder.*[1]

Women are likewise eligible to the office of guardian of the poor. The absence of any express statutory provision has given rise to doubt, but in practice the question has been settled in favour of the eligibility of women to the Board of Guardians.[2]

Under the guardians of the poor, there are in every parish overseers of the poor. This office though representative is not elective. The overseers are appointed every year from among the "substantial householders" by the justices of the peace. Judicial opinion,[3] supported by long usage, has decided that women can be invested with these duties.

(4) Just as the parishes and the unions are independent of the rural and urban districts in which they are comprised or which they intersect, so the towns form separate units of local government, and are by no means alike in their organisation. A certain number of towns occupy a privileged position under the name of "municipal boroughs." These alone

[1] Compare E. Eiloart, "The Law Relating to Women." London, 1878, p. 19.

[2] *Ibid.*

[3] Rex *v.* Stubbs (1787), 2 Durnford and East, 395.

are municipal corporations, enjoying a considerable degree of autonomy by virtue of charters of incorporation granted at the pleasure of the Crown. Of the thousand urban agglomerations with more than 2000 inhabitants, only a fourth part have the rank of municipal boroughs; all the other towns have as such no legal existence, they are simply geographical units.[1] In past times the privilege of incorporation was frequently granted to wretched little hamlets. But whether they were once of consequence or not, municipal corporations everywhere degenerated into corrupt oligarchies. The Municipal Reform of 1835 broke up these hereditary coteries, and extended the municipal franchise to all the inhabitants who paid poor rates as occupiers of realty. In consequence of this, the number of municipal electors was to be so considerably increased, and they were to possess so extensive an autonomy (including the control of the police), that the legislator thought it hardly expedient to take in as voters all the ratepayers, irrespective of sex, as was the practice in the primary stage of local government, in the parish. So it was expressly provided in the Municipal Corporations Act of 1835 that the franchise in municipal boroughs should belong to male persons only.[2]

The unorganised condition of the towns which were not municipal boroughs received before long the attention of the legislator, who granted them not local autonomy—there could be no question about that—but special powers for the establishment of sanitary systems and the execution of works of public utility,

[1] As stated by Chalmers in the work cited, p. 62.

[2] 5 and 6 Will. IV., c. 79, sec. 9.

such as lighting, paving, sewerage, etc. The special Acts of Parliament passed for this purpose, as the necessity for them arose, were consolidated in two general Acts—the Public Health Act of 1848, for a class of towns termed "local government districts," and the Commissioners Clauses Act of 1847, for the towns which were surnamed "improvement commissions." These statutes conferred on these urban agglomerations an incipient municipal organisation, by establishing in the one set Boards of Health, and in the other Commissioners, to direct the works of public utility. In both these classes of "nascent and half-developed municipalities,"[1] which had scarcely emerged from the parochial stage of local self-government, the authorities, that is, the members of the Boards of Health and the Commissioners, were elected by the ratepayers, as in the parishes, without distinction of sex.

As these towns enlarged and developed, they were admitted to the privilege of municipal incorporation. But since the Municipal Corporation Act limited the franchise to men, it came to pass that when a town was promoted to the rank of a municipal borough, and saw its rights increased, a part of its inhabitants, *viz.*, the women, saw theirs suppressed. This anomaly gave the supporters of Women's Suffrage a strong argument for insisting that the vote should be granted to women in municipal boroughs.[2] In 1869,

[1] Geo. Brodrick, "Local Government in England." Cobden Clu Essays on Local Government, ed. by Probyn. London, 1882, p. 38.

[2] In 1869 there were 78 non-corporate towns in which women had the right of voting.

Mr. Jacob Bright moved a resolution to this effect in the House of Commons, and it was adopted almost without debate;[1] so evident was the justice of their cause, as said and say still the advocates of Women's Suffrage. But, on the other hand, it may be pointed out that the House had refused before 1869 (and was going to refuse after 1869), to give women the parliamentary suffrage, although this was demanded under the same conditions as those under which the municipal franchise had been granted to them. Indeed, the fact that the legislator has expressly excluded women from the suffrage in the Municipal Corporations Act, while leaving them in possession of it in parochial administration, allows but little doubt that he meant to draw in this regard a distinction between the elementary sphere of local interests and the higher spheres of self-government. In the same spirit a distinction has been established, as we shall see, in Germany between towns and country districts. But when the English legislator assimilated the "nascent, half-developed municipalities," which were only temporarily such and might become cities of the first rank, to the parishes, so far as regards woman's vote, he introduced a fluctuating instead of a fixed test, and as a result wiped out his own line of demarcation. When this fact was brought out, Parliament could not but admit and bow to it. This admission was decisive; it swept away the electoral barriers which had been raised against women in the entire domain of self-government.

The clause adopted on the motion of Mr. Jacob Bright, and introduced in the Municipal Act of 1869

[1] Hansard, vol. cxcvi., Appendix, 7th June, 1869.

(32 and 33 Vict., c. 55, Section 9), has been incorporated in the revised Municipal Act of 1882, Section 63, in the following terms :—" For all purposes connected with and having reference to the right to vote at municipal elections, words importing in this Act the masculine gender include women."[1] This clause granted to women in municipal boroughs the right to vote but not the right to be elected. And as the general qualification for municipal suffrage is the occupancy by the electors, in their own name, of a house rated to the poor tax, only independent women, unmarried, benefited by the Act. There could be no doubt as to them. But how about the married woman who was separated from her husband, and kept house herself, in respect of which she paid rates? The Court of Queen's Bench decided in 1872 in the case of Regina *v.* Harrald, that a woman who was neither widow nor spinster, was excluded from the municipal suffrage, for, as the Lord Chief Justice said, the legislature only intended to remedy the injustice which was done to the woman who paid the rates and did not get the vote, but it did not intend to change the *status* of the married women, which were merged in their husbands according to the common law.[2] The Court felt more doubt as to whether a woman whose name was placed on the annual list of electors at a time when she was not married, would lose the right to vote if she married subsequently.[3]

When the municipal suffrage was extended to women in Scotland in 1881, the question of the right of a

[1] 45 and 46 Vict., c. 50.

[2] The Law Rep., vii., Q.B., 363 (1872).

[3] See the opinion of Mr. Justice Hannen, *ibid*, p. 364.

woman, separated from her husband, to vote, was decided in her favour.[1] But, of course, this does not affect the position of women separated from their husbands in England.

(5) A year after the introduction of the municipal suffrage of women, they obtained (in 1870) the School Board vote also, in connection with the establishment of the present system of elementary education. Before 1870, nearly all the primary schools were private institutions supported by private endowments belonging generally to the various religious bodies. The Act of 1870 provided that in districts where the Education Department, or the ratepayers themselves, might find it necessary to establish public schools, there should be formed to superintend them a School Committee or School Board, consisting of 5 to 15 members, elected by the usual electors of the municipal boroughs or parishes,[2] that is, including women, except in the "city" of London. In that part of London the members of the School Board are chosen by those who have a vote for the common councilmen,[3] in accordance with the peculiar constitution of the city, and this right pertains only to males.[4] The qualifications for eligibility to these Boards not having been determined by law, it has been interpreted in the widest sense. No one is excluded. Women, whether married or unmarried, are eligible. The general order of the Education Department has placed no restriction but the qualification of age. [5]

[1] 44 Vict., c. 13, sec. 2.
[2] 33 and 34 Vict., c. 73, sec. 29.
[3] *Ibid*, sec. 37, sub-sec. 6.
[4] 12 and 13 Vict., c. 94, and 30 and 31 Vict., c. 1.
[5] "The Elementary Education Acts," 1870-1880, by Hugh Owen, (16 edit., London, 1884) p. 112,

(6) It still remained for women to obtain access to the self-government of the county ; but if county government was representative, it was nowhere elective. Only in 1888, County Councils elected by the ratepayers were formed. In pursuance of the system already in force, women could not but be included among the electors of the new local assemblies. Both the Local Government Act of 1888 [1] in England, and the Act of 1889 [2] in Scotland, admited women to the electorate.

These Acts have borrowed from the respective Municipal Acts the provisions for Female Suffrage; so that in England married women, though separated from their husbands, are ineligible, whilst in Scotland the law gives the vote to "every woman who is not married and living in family with her husband." [3]

The eligibility to County Councils being subject by the Act of 1888 (sec. 2) to the same conditions which are in force for Municipal Councils, women are thereby excluded. Nevertheless, some of them assumed that they were eligible, and presented themselves to the electors as candidates. The widow of Lord Sandhurst and the daughter of the illustrious Cobden were elected in London. The London County Council, on its part, having to choose county aldermen,[4] elected a woman as one of them. But before long the right of these women to sit and vote was tested in the Courts. Lady Sandhurst's

[1] 51 and 52 Vict., c. 41, and 57 Vict., c. (County Electors Act), sec. 2.

[2] 52 and 53 Vict., c. 50.

[3] 52 and 53 Vict., c. 50, sec. 28, sub-sec. 2, i.

[4] Two-thirds of the municipal councillors and the county councillors are elected by the inhabitants for three years, and the council select the remaining one-third (aldermen) for six years.

defeated opponent asked the Court to decide that the votes received by her were null, as given to a person who had not the necessary legal capacity, and to declare him elected for the division. The Court gave judgment for the claimant. Then the case was taken by the defendant to the Court of Appeal, but the decision given by the Court of first instance was confirmed. The defendant's plea rested on the fact that the law (Sec. 11 of the Municipal Act of 1882) declared eligible all those who at the time of the election were qualified to elect councillors, and that as the Act did not contain any words specially excluding women, they ought to enjoy the same right to be elected as any other elector. The Lord Chief Justice, who presided over the Court of Appeal,[1] in the judgment which he delivered, expressed the opinion that, if there had been no other provision upon the matter but Section 11 of the Act of 1882, it would, if interpreted in accordance to Lord Brougham's Act, have conferred on women the right to be elected, but that as Section 63 limited the right of women to voting at the elections, they had no right to be elected. Among the other members of the High Court who gave their opinion in this case, the Master of the Rolls seems to me to have approached nearest to the judicial principle which should really govern the decision. He did so in alluding to the case of Chorlton *v.* Lings, and in explaining that it says this: "Women being excluded under the common law of England, when you have a statute which deals with public functions, unless that statute

[1] And who in 1868 argued in favour of the parliamentary suffrage of women, as Counsel for the lady appellant in the case of Chorlton *v.* Lings.

expressly gives power to women to exercise them, it is to be taken that the true construction is that the powers given are confined to men, and that Lord Brougham's Act does not apply."[1]

The two other female members of the London County Council, without resigning, absented themselves from the Council, to resume their seats a year later, hoping to be able to avail themselves of Clause 73 of the Act of 1882, in accordance with which the validity of an election cannot be disputed after the expiration of twelve months. But one of their male colleagues, whose keen sense of legality revolted against seeing at the Council persons who had no right to sit there, brought an action against one of these ladies, for the recovery of a penalty of £50 for each of the five times which she had voted in the Council. The Queen's Bench Division found extenuating circumstances, and condemned the lady defendant to pay only £25 for each vote. The Court of Appeal was still more lenient, and taxed each vote at ten shillings.[2]

In the Local Government Act for Scotland, passed a year later than that for England, the legislator took care to insert a formal clause declaring women ineligible to the County Councils.[3]

Before passing to the countries of the Continent, it ought to be observed that all the provisions analysed above relate to Great Britain only, that is, to England and Wales and Scotland, but not to Ireland. In this latter country women enjoy no electoral rights either in the parishes, the municipalities, or in the counties.

[1] Beresford *v.* Lady Sandhurst, L.R. 23, Q.B.D. 79 (1889).

[2] De Souza *v.* Cobden, L.R.. 1 Q.B., 687, (1891).

[3] 52 and 53 Vict., c. 50, sec. 9.

There are only a few unimportant exceptions to this. For instance, women are admitted to vote in the town of Belfast for Harbour Commissioners, and in some other places for Town Commissioners,[1] but that is all.[2]

§ 3.—Scandinavia and Finland.

(1) In Sweden local self-government is, in the first instance, administered in the urban and rural communes by the general assembly of the ratepayers, where their votes count in proportion to the amount of their rates, according to a graded scale, as in the English vestries. In towns with a population of more than 3000 inhabitants, the ratepayers, as a rule, elect a communal council. In towns of less importance, as well as in the rural communes, the election of a council is optional. The executive organs of the commune are appointed by the general assembly, and where its powers are delegated to a council, by the council. Unmarried women take part equally with men in the full assemblies of the communes which have no councils, and in the elections for the appointment of those councils. They can vote in person, or, making use of a right that is general, by proxy.[3]

The next stage of local self-government consists of

[1] Compare "Woman Suffrage," by Mrs. Ashton Dilke (London, 1885), pp. 83, 85.

[2] In one of the Channel Islands, in Guernsey, women are allowed since October 31, 1891, to take part in parochial elections.

[3] The Communal Law of March 21, 1862: as regards the rural communes, §§ 14, 29 and 42; as regards the towns, except Stockholm, §§ 29 and 56; the law of May 23, 1872, § 5, and of August 27, 1883, on the municipal organization of Stockholm.

the provincial councils (landstings). The members of these councils are elected by the municipal voters, including the women. In the towns the election is direct, and in the rural communes it is indirect, through electors. The landstings, in concert with the communal councils of the large towns, in their turn elect the members of the Upper House, as I have already explained in the last chapter. While they take part in the full communal assemblies, and possess the municipal vote in the first instance, women are not capable of being elected. Two exceptions have been established in this respect by two recent laws of the 22nd March, 1889. The first of these laws made women eligible for Municipal Poor-relief Committees throughout the whole kingdom, and the second allowed them to be appointed to the School Board for Stockholm.

(2) In Norway, women have no share in local government, except in school administration, as defined by the law of the 26th June, 1889. In the towns they are eligible for the School Boards, which direct the public schools. The members of these Boards are generally chosen by the municipal council.[1] Those women who have children can vote for inspectors. In the rural communes the women have more extensive rights. Every rural municipality is divided for purposes of school administration into districts; every district has its assembly, to vote supplies, decide upon other educational matters, and appoint the inspectors. At these assemblies all persons who pay the school tax take part, women and men. In deciding questions not relating to expenditure, the parents, fathers and mothers alike, are

[1] §§ 40 and 47 of the law of June 26, 1889.

also admitted, even though they contribute nothing to the school funds. Women are eligible to the post of inspectors.[1]

(3) In Denmark, women are entirely excluded from local government, but they have been admitted to it in one Danish dependency—in Iceland. This island in the glacial Arctic Ocean, with a population of 75,000 inhabitants, is governed by an independent legislative assembly (Althing), under the sovereignty of the King of Denmark. For local administration purposes Iceland is divided into twenty-two districts (sysler), which, in their turn, are sub-divided into cantons or communes (hrapper). The head magistrates of these administrative divisions are appointed by the electors, who possess the requisite property qualification. The law of 12th May, 1882, conferred on women the right to take part in these elections, as well as in parish meetings for church affairs. The law thus describes the qualification of female voters: "Widows and other unmarried women who have an establishment of their own, or otherwise occupy an independent position."[2]

(4) Finland, which was attached to Sweden for centuries before it became a Russian dependency, is still influenced by the legislative movement of its old mother country. Soon after the establishment of the Swedish municipal organisation that we have just analysed, Finland reformed its own. The law of 6th February, 1865, concerning rural communes, admitted women to communal rights under almost the same conditions as in Sweden. The communal administration of

[1] §§ 47, 53, 54.

[2] "Annuaire de législ. comp.," XIII., 820.

Finnish rural districts is vested, as in Sweden, in the general assembly of ratepayers (Communalstämma), and, in the second place, in executive committees (Communal-nâmnd) elected in the general assemblies. Widowed, divorced and unmarried women, have the right to vote at these assemblies.

The municipal government of towns was, until quite recently, in the hands of corporations of the "burghers," who have shown the same narrow and exclusive spirit in Finland as elsewhere. The law of the 8th December, 1873, put an end to this oligarchical rule, and conferred communal rights on all the ratepayers—men and women. Every woman "mistress of her person and her property," that is to say, every widowed, divorced or unmarried woman, enjoys the right to take part in the deliberations of the communal assembly (Râdhusstamma), both in towns of less than 2000 inhabitants, where there is direct municipal government, and also at the election of representatives (Stadsfullmœktige) in towns where the deliberative powers of the general assembly are delegated to a council. The votes have always a relative value, proportionate to the amount of the rates paid by the elector.

Eligibility to the post of town representative, as also to the office of member of the communal executive committee in the rural districts, is limited to men.[1] But a recent law of the 6th August, 1889, made women eligible to the office of guardian of the poor in towns, and also in rural districts, where similar offices exist apart from the communal committees (Communalnâmnd).

[1] § 27 of the law of 1873 relating to the organisation of towns § 43 and 13 of the law of 1865 relating to rural communes.

§ 4.—Germany and Austria.

(1) In paragraph 1 of this chapter I endeavoured to show that whenever communal law, taking property as the criterion, and eliminating the personal element, has admitted women to the municipal suffrage, it has at the same time, as far as they are concerned, drawn a line of demarcation between those organs of local self-government which are essentially of a private character, and those which, owing to the complexity of the public functions entrusted to them, more nearly approach in activity the State itself.

In England, the local franchise of women, which was at first limited to the parish vote, was subsequently extended in consequence of exceptional circumstances which I have detailed. In Sweden, Finland, and Iceland, where there are very few large towns, and the difference between the urban and rural communes is much less marked than elsewhere (we saw that both were governed directly by general assemblies), women have been admitted to communal rights in the towns as well as in the rural districts. In Germany, where the contrast between the town municipalities and the rural communes is very pronounced, we, for the first time, see the line of demarcation between the two, in respect of the enjoyment of the communal right, clearly defined and sharply maintained. Women are admitted to the municipal suffrage in the country, but universally excluded in the towns.

It is in this way that the question is settled in Prussia and particularly in the six eastern provinces, where side by side with towns possessing a considerable municipal autonomy with extensive powers, are found rural communes (Landgemeinden), which are "essentially private corporations, associations for economic purposes, to which a minimum of public authority has been delegated from geographical necessity."[1] These communes have no police jurisdiction, do not coincide with the other administrative divisions of a public character, and appear simply as "closely-packed villages, situated in the centre of a parcelled-out agricultural area, which, till a very late date, was cultivated in common on the three-field system."[2] The law of the 14th April, 1856, on the organisation of the rural communes of the six eastern provinces of the kingdom of Prussia (Sec. 6), as well as the analogous law of the 19th March, 1856, for the province of Westphalia (Sec. 15) provides that persons of the female sex, who possess real property, carrying with it the right to vote, shall be represented for this purpose—the married women by their husbands, and unmarried women by electors of the male sex. A similar arrangement was adopted subsequently for the province of Schleswig-Holstein after its annexation to Prussia (Sec. 11 of the law of the 22nd September, 1867),[3] But in the Rhine province, the administrative and civil legislation of which still bears well-marked traces of French influence, women are expressly excluded from the communal franchise. Paragraph 35 of the law of the 23rd July, 1845, modified on 15th May, 1856, declares

[1] Sir Robert Morier, "Local Government in England and Germany: An Essay reprinted from the Cobden Club Series on Local Government." London, 1888, p. 71.

[2] *Ibid*, p. 72.

[3] The new law on the organisation of the rural communes of the seven eastern provinces, of June 3, 1891, has not made any change in regard to the female vote (*Cf.* §§ 45, 46 and 53).

that communal rights (das Gemeinderecht) can only be exercised by those of the male sex who are highest rated (these alone were electors at that period).[1]

To a certain extent women take part equally with men in the elections for the cantonal assemblies, the diets of the rural circles (Kreistag), the members of which are elected, (1) by the large rural landowners, the proprietors of factories and mines taxed on the higher scale, in respect of the industries which they carry on in the open country, within the limits of the circle; (2) by the independent landowners and manufacturers taxed on the lower scale in respect of the said industries, and by the representatives of the rural communes; (3) by the towns, if there are any in the rural circle. This organisation, which reminds one of that of the Austrian provinces, equally grants to men and women the right of representation in the group of large proprietors with its two sub-divisions, the members of which take part in the elections in their own name. Unmarried women vote by mandatories chosen by them from among proprietors of the circle.[2] The votes of women of this category extend to the provincial assemblies (Provinziallandtage), these last being composed of deputies from the rural circles, appointed by their respective diets, and of representatives of large towns.

In Brunswick, the law of the 17th March, 1850, relating to the rural communes, enacts that the vote must be given by the elector in person, but that by way of

[1] For the text of all these communal laws see Stœppel's "Preussisch-Deutscher Gesetz-Codex," in 6 volumes. Hamburg, 1882.

[2] Law of the 13th December, 1872, on the organisation of Circles, Secs. 97, 98. "Annuaire," II., 308, 309.

exception, unmarried women (widows or spinsters) may vote by proxy. The sons, sons-in-law, or step-sons who are delegated by women for this purpose, are not required to present a formal power of attorney (Sec. 23).[1]

Lastly, in Saxony, women are admitted to the communal vote in the rural districts on the same terms as men. Paragraph 34 of the law of the 24th April, 1873,[2] gives the franchise "to every member of the commune except non-resident women" who are in possession of real property, etc., in the commune. Married women are represented at the poll by their husbands, single women vote in person (Sec. 16). The old communal law of the 7th November, 1838 (Sec. 30), went so far as to provide expressly that husbands should vote for their wives only in case they were not separated in *bed and board*.[3]

Eligibility to communal offices is denied to women in all the above named countries.[4]

(2) In Austria, the legislator, in consequence of the commotion of 1848, anxious to revive local life, granted a liberal organisation to the rural communes. He admitted to communal rights all persons paying taxes on realty and industrial enterprises, and also to different categories of persons having an educational qualification, such as ministers of religion, university graduates, principals of schools, and teachers of the higher grades, etc.

[1] Gesetz-und-Verordnungs-Sammlung für die Herzoglich Braunschveigischen Lande, 37 Jahrgang, 1850.

[2] Landgemeindeordnung für das Königreich Sachsen (Gesetz-und-Verordnungsblatt vom Jahre 1873. Dresden.)

[3] The same collection, 1838.

[4] Sec. 17 of the Law of Brunswick of 1850; Sec. 37 of the Law of Saxony of 1873.

Among the electors of the first and most important group, which was formed exclusively on the basis of property, women, minors, military men in active service, and some other categories of persons generally excluded from the suffrage, were included on condition of their voting by proxy.[1] The fourth article of the Communal Code in force [2] provides, as regards women, that "the wife living in matrimony exercises her electoral right through her husband, women who are independent (*sui juris*) by proxy, persons not *sui juris* by their legal representatives." As the last clause of the article makes no reservation as to the sex of the "person not *sui juris*," female minors are also included. On the other hand, women separated from their husbands, not being "wives living in matrimony," enjoy the franchise, if they are of age, on the same terms as unmarried women *sui juris*.[3] The ordinances of Bohemia and Upper Austria are silent as regards married women. In Moravia, where we have already had occasion to appreciate the liberality of legislative provisions in regard to women, the law gives, even to a married woman, the right to be represented

[1] A legislative movement has lately been started for granting to women the right to give their communal vote in person. The diet of Lower Austria passed, on the 3rd January, 1891, a clause to this effect.

[2] Uebereinstimmende Anordnungen der Gemeinde-Wahlordnungen, the Statutes of the 5th March, 1862, which took the place of the Provisional Communal Law of the 17th March, 1849. (Allgemeines Reichsgesetz und Regierungsblatt fur das Kaiserreich Oesterreich.)

[3] The Communal Law, in its earlier form (that of 1849), was more explicit on this subject. It declared that "widows and women divorced from their husbands or unmarried, should vote by proxy," Sec. 30.

by a proxy of her own choice, in case the husband is disqualified from voting (on account of his being deprived of civil rights, etc.). The Moravian law is thus more liberal than the law of Saxony, which expressly stipulates that in such cases the electoral right of the woman is suspended.[1]

The suffrage granted to persons qualified on account of their educational standard appears to be limited to men: that is implied in the decision, already cited, of the Supreme Court with regard to the female teachers of Moravia.

Eligibility to the executive committees is expressly limited in all the Austrian provinces to men (§ 10 of the Law of Bohemia, § 9 of the ordinances of the other provinces).

In the municipal organisation of the towns, based principally on the communal laws of 1849 and 1862, the legislator has not seen fit to admit the principle of representation, so that women, minors, etc., are excluded from the municipal suffrage in the towns.[2]

As to the Transleithanian part of the Habsburg Empire, women are absolutely excluded from local government in Hungary, while in Croatia-Slavonia[3] they may vote, by proxy, for town councils, except in those towns which are within the former Land of the Military Borders.[4]

1 ". . . so ruht das Stimmrecht" (§ 36 of the Revidirte Landgemeindeordnung für das Königreich Sachsen, 1873).

2 Das Gemeindegesetz of 5th March, 1862; Manzsche Gesetzausgabe, (Wien, 1875), t. ix., p. 288.

3 §§ 22, 25, and 26 of the law of January 28, 1882, on the organisation of urban communes.

4 Order of the Ban (viceroy) of Croatia, etc., No. 20517.

§ 5.—Russia.

(1) The Russian village community—the *mir*,—which has survived through centuries down to our times, with very little change in its primitive organisation, presents us with a typical instance of rudimentary local self-government, where *all* those who have an interest, not excepting women, have their say in the communal assemblies. The Russian legislator, who is, as a rule, not loth to issue regulations, has been very moderate in his provisions regarding the *mir*. He has simply recognised the established custom in declaring that "the rural assembly is composed of the peasant householders belonging to the rural community, and of all the rural officers appointed by election. The householder is not forbidden, in case of absence, or illness, or generally in case of inability to attend personally at the assembly, to send a member of his family in his place."[1] This right of representation is often exercised by a widow, and even by a married woman, especially in the poor provinces, where a considerable portion of the male population of the country districts is obliged to go and find work at a distance. As representatives of the families or households, women enjoy the same rights in the village assemblies as the men.[2]

[1] Code of Laws of the Russian Empire, t. ii., art. 2191.

[2] "In matters affecting the general welfare of the community they rarely speak, and if they do venture to enunciate an opinion on such occasions, they have little chance of commanding attention, for the Russian peasantry are as yet little imbued with the modern doctrines of female equality, and express their opinion of female

(2) In the *mir* assemblies only the peasants, *i.e.*, persons who belong to *the peasant order*, take part. The other classes of the population exercise local self-government (the only self-government known in Russia) by means of "territorial assemblies," composed of representatives of all classes. The members of these assemblies are elected partly by direct suffrage, partly through electors, by the owners of real property (whether individuals or corporate persons) grouped for this purpose in electoral colleges, according to their social status, and also by the rural peasant communities. Every district has its territorial assembly. Delegates from the district assemblies form the provincial assembly which corresponds more or less to the English county council, or to the *conseil général* in France.

intelligence by the homely adage, "The hair is long, but the mind is short." According to one proverb, seven women have collectively but one soul; and, according to a still more ungallant popular saying, women have no souls at all, but only a vapour. Woman, therefore, as a woman, is not deserving of much consideration, but a particular woman, as head of a household, is entitled to speak on all questions directly affecting the household under her care. If, for instance, it be proposed to increase or diminish her household's share of the land and the burdens, she will be allowed to speak freely on the subject, and even indulge in a little personal invective against her male opponents. She thereby exposes herself, it is true, to uncomplimentary remarks; but any which she happens to receive she will probably repay with interest, referring, perhaps, with a pertinent virulence to the domestic affairs of those who attack her. And where arguments and invectives fail, she is pretty sure to try the effect of a pathetic appeal, supported by copious tears, a method of persuasion to which the Russian peasant is singularly insensible" ("Russia," by Sir Donald Mackenzie Wallace. London, 1887. p. 129).

Married and unmarried women are allowed to vote by proxy for the members of the territorial assemblies of the district, or for the electors, who are to choose them. They can delegate as proxies their fathers, husbands, sons, sons-in-law, grandsons, brothers, or nephews, even when such persons do not themselves possess the requisite property qualifications.[1] It will be at once observed that married women are as free to choose their delegates as are the unmarried women; they can pass over their husbands in favour of their fathers, nephews, etc. In the next place, it is worthy of note that before 1890[2] the woman could choose her proxy from among all male persons who had the right of voting in the electoral college.[3]

In urban self-government, which is exercised by councils elected by the various classes of ratepayers, women have a vote on the same terms as for the "territorial assemblies."[4] Here too women were allowed, under the old municipal statute (of 1870), to select as male proxies whom they chose, but the new law has limited the range of proxies to near relatives, just as it did in respect of the "territorial" vote.

(3) As elective local government in Russia begins with the lowest "order" in the State, *viz.*, the peasants, so it ends with the self-government of the highest "order," the nobility. Since the reforms of Alexander II. the

[1] Statute on territorial institutions of the 12th June, 1890, art. 18, 21.

[2] The charter of local self-government granted by Alexander II., in 1864, has been replaced by the statute of 1890.

[3] Russian Code, t. ii., art. 1834.

[4] Municipal Statute of 11th June, 1892, sects. 25, 26, and 28.

body of the nobility has scarcely any political importance; it is rather a corporation with interests of a private character, such as the guardianship of persons of noble birth and the assistance of orphans. The marshal of the nobility, elected in a general assembly of the order of nobles, presides *ex officio* over the "territorial" assembly and over various other administrative councils, and it is only through him that the nobility can make its influence legally felt in local self-government.

The woman of noble birth who owns property, carrying with it the right to take part in the elections of the order, can transfer her right to her husband, son, or son-in-law, even if such persons do not possess the requisite property qualification. In default of the above-mentioned relatives, or in case of their being unable to act, she can delegate her vote to a stranger, either her full right or simply the right to take part in the elections without joining in the deliberations and other decisions of the assembly.[1]

Since we began the study of woman's place in local self-government, it is for the first time (if we except the Austrian province of Moravia) that we meet with anything like this public emancipation of married women. In the great Slavic empire this fact is simply a consequence of the civil *status* of the married woman, who there enjoys all the rights of a *feme sole*, to use the Anglo-Norman term. The various elective bodies of Russia, noticed above, being deprived of any political character, by the peculiar constitution of the empire of the Tzars, if for no other reason, and having only the charge of economic interests, the married woman, eman-

[1] *Ibid*, vol. ix., art. 111, 125,

cipated by the Civil Code, simply carries her civil *status* with her when she enters the sphere of local self-government as a landowner and taxpayer.

(4) Thus we find that in the Germanic and in the Slavic world, where the right to take part in local self-government does not depend on being a citizen or a member of the body politic, but on having a stake in the land or at least on being a substantial taxpayer, the woman is often, if not always, admitted on this ground to the local suffrage. On the other hand, in the Latin world, where communal right coincides or nearly coincides with political citizenship, the woman is invariably excluded from all share in the management of common affairs. (Attempts made and frequently repeated in Italy to confer on women the "administrative suffrage" have come to nothing.) A country, at once Latin and Germanic —Switzerland, whose Romanic and Germanic cantons exemplify pretty well the general difference alluded to of the two kinds of municipal organisation, confirmed and completed to a certain extent that contrast by the different attitudes of the legislators of the several cantons with regard to the admission of woman to local administration. Whilst in the cantons of Geneva and Vaud women were excluded, the municipal law of the canton of Berne, of the 6th December, 1852, gave vote by proxy to independent women liable to the payment of the communal tax (Art. 22). The Bernese women at first made no use of this right, but in 1885, at the instigation of the rival parties, they descended into the fray to support the one or the other side. In this instance the assumption that women's votes represented only economic interests of which they had charge, proved false; their

right to vote at municipal elections, whilst they were still excluded from the political suffrage, consequently appeared incongruous, and after the election, in which they had for the first time made use of their franchise, it was taken from them.

§ 6.—Non-European Countries.

The non-European countries in which the question of the participation of women in local self-government has been raised are the English Colonies and the United States of America.

(1) In the English Colonies the question has been decided in the same way as in the mother country, that is to say, that independent women, who are ratepayers, are allowed to vote at the local elections. As in the mother country, the vote is generally attached to the possession or occupation of real property, and votes count in proportion to the rateable value of lands or houses. In the Dominion of Canada local suffrage has only recently been granted to women. The first law on the subject was passed in the province of Ontario (Upper Canada) in 1884. This law has served as an example and partly as a model for the other provinces. The electoral rights given to women by the legislation of Ontario may be grouped under four heads:—(1) to take part in municipal elections; (2) to vote in case a bye-law requires the assent of the electors of a municipality before the final passage thereof; (3) to vote on school questions and at elections for school trustees; (4) to be elected school trustees. In the municipal elections, as well as in voting on a bye-law which requires the assent of the electors,

the vote belongs to all unmarried women or widows being of the age of twenty-one years, subjects of Her Majesty, and rated on the assessment roll for real property held in their own right or for income.[1] In the elections for school trustees, and at the meetings held to decide all other matters relating to the schools, every taxpayer who contributes to the maintenance of the public schools is entitled to vote,[2] whilst women were already in possession of a vote for school trustees in 1850. As to their eligibility to the office of school trustee, the laws of 1885 and 1887 (48 Vic., c. 49, sec. 107, and 50 Vic., c. 39, sec. 23) have recognised that right as pertaining to every resident ratepayer within the school section.[3]

In the other provinces of Canada, local suffrage has been granted to women under still more liberal conditions. So in Nova Scotia the vote is given even to married women, whose husbands have no right to vote.[4] In British Columbia and Manitoba the suffrage is granted to all married women who are of age.[5] Lastly, in the North West Territory the municipal franchise is conferred on widows and unmarried women.[6] Female Suffrage does not exist in the great French-speaking province of Quebec (Lower Canada), nor in New Brunswick, nor in Prince Edward's Island.

[1] The Revised Statutes of Ontario (1887), c. 184, part iii. title i., div. 1, secs. 79 and 308.

[2] *Ibid*, c. 225., sec. 14.

[3] *Ibid*, sec. 13, 106.

[4] Law of the 3rd May, 1887 (Statutes 1887, c. 28).

[5] Revised Statutes of British Columbia (1888), c. 88 ; Statutes of 1889, c. 34 ; Statutes of 1890, c. 34, secs. 12, 13 ; Statutes of Manitoba (1887), c. 10 (Law of the 10th June, 1887).

[6] Revised Ordinances of 1888, c. 8., secs. 18 and 19.

In Australasia, municipal suffrage has been introduced in all the colonies of the Continent[1] on the basis of the parochial franchise of the mother country. That is to say, by making the municipal vote dependent on the possession or occupation of real property, and by graduating the value of the vote according to the amount of the rates paid, the law has made no distinction of sex between the ratepaying voters.

In New Zealand, women enjoy the right to vote at all the local elections on the same conditions.[2] In Tasmania (formerly known as Van Dieman's Land), the suffrage was at first limited to men; but an Act of 1884 extended it in rural municipalities to women, on the same conditions both as to property qualifications and as to plurality of votes,[3] as in other parts of Australasia.

(2) Very different is the state of the question of female municipal suffrage in the United States. In spite of the liveliest agitation, women have not succeeded in obtaining the suffrage, and still less the right to be elected to office. They secured the municipal vote in a single State only, in Kansas. (We except of course the State of Wyoming, where women have obtained the municipal vote, as one of the consequences of their political emancipation.) An Act of 1887 grants to women in Kansas the right to vote in cities of the first, second, and third classes, at any election of city or school officers, or for

[1] Law of 1867 in New South Wales; Municipal Law of 1869 (revised in 1875) in Victoria; Municipal Law of 1871 (revised statutes of 1883) in Western Australia; Municipal Law of 1880 in South Australia.

[2] The Municipal Corporations Act of 1886; the Counties Act of the same year, etc.

[3] The Rural Municipalities Amendment Act (1884), sec. 4.

the purpose of authorising the issue of bonds for school purposes; and any woman qualified to vote has also the right to be elected to the said offices.[1] In other States the proposal to extend the municipal suffrage of women, though frequently brought forward, has been rejected.[2] Resistance to it is particularly strong in the States of New England, which were the cradle of American liberty and the birth-place of the Great Republic. Traditions which are wholly non-existent in the mushroom Western States, have still some weight in the Eastern States. As municipal suffrage is no longer dependent on a property qualification throughout nearly the whole of the Union, its extension to women stands on the same footing as the concession of a political vote, and meets with the same resistance.[3]

[1] Session Laws of 1887, c. 230 (Law of the 15th February, 1887).

[2] In one of these States, in Michigan, the Women's Suffrage advocates have just succeeded in obtaining for them, after ten years of persistent effort, the municipal franchise on the condition of an educational qualification. In consequence of the law of May 27, 1893, "women who are able to read the Constitution of the State of Michigan, printed in the English language, shall be allowed to vote for all school, village, and city officers, and on all questions pertaining to school, village, and city regulations, on the same terms and conditions prescribed by law for male citizens. Before any woman shall be registered as a voter, the Board of Registration shall require her to read, in the presence of said Board, at least one section of the Constitution of this State in the English language."

[3] *Cf.* the discussion of the Female Suffrage Bill in the Massachusetts Legislature in 1878. While the members of the committee, to which the Bill was referred, have disclosed irreconcilable divergencies of opinion on the general question of Woman Suffrage, they were unanimous in declaring that if the suffrage was dependent on a property qualification, there would have been no difficulty in

But several States, while refusing to grant women a vote, as a general rule, in the sphere of local self-government, or in that of State Government, have admitted women to one particular branch administered by elective assemblies, *viz.*, that of the primary public schools. The electors, or those who contribute to the maintenance of the schools, choose annually the members of the school committees and the superintendent for the county, and vote the expenses and the taxes or loans required to defray them. Several States have granted to women simply the right to be elected to school offices, so that only certain women picked out by the electors on account of their personal merit are allowed to step into the sphere of local administration. This was the way the question was settled in the States of California, Illinois, Indiana, Iowa, Louisiana, Maine, Pennsylvania and Rhode Island.[1] Massachusetts at first adopted the same line of policy, declaring that no person should be considered ineligible to the school board by reason of sex,[2] but later this State granted to women also the

extending it to women ("Appleton's Annual Cyclopædia," 1878, p. 525).

[1] Political Code of California, sec. 1593, par. 1 as amended April 7, 1880 (Statutes of 1880, c. 80, sec. 14); Revised Statutes of Illinois (1874), c. 122, secs. 98, 99 (Law of April 3, 1873); Revised Statutes of Indiana (1881), sec. 4540 (Law of April 14, 1881); Acts of Iowa, 1876, c. 136 (Law of March 17, 1876); Constitution of Louisiana (1879), art. 232; Revised Statutes of Maine (1883), tit. ii., c. 11, sec. 18 (Law of Feb. 26, 1881); Constitution of Pennsylvania (1873), art. 10, sec. 3; Constitution of Rhode Island, art. 9, sec. 1, and Public Statutes (1882), c. 50, sec. 54.

[2] Public Statutes of Massachusetts (1882), c. 44, sec. 21 (Law of June 30, 1874).

right to vote for the members of these boards.[1] Some other States have proceeded in the same manner.

At the present time the system which confers on women both the right to be elected and the right of election at school boards has been adopted in the following States, besides Massachusetts: Colorado, North and South Dakota, Idaho, Michigan, Minnesota, Montana, New Hampshire, New Jersey, New York, Oregon, Vermont, Washington and Wisconsin, and the Territory of Arizona.[2] Of course, there must also be added to this list

[1] *Ibid*, c. 6, sec. 3 (Laws of April 16, 1879, and of April 7, 1881). Cf. also Acts 1884, c. 298, sec. 4; 1887, c. 249, sec. 1; 1888, c. 426, secs. 4, 10.

[2] General Statutes of Colorado (1883), c. 97, sec. 45, and Constitution (1876), art. 7, sec. 1; Constitution of North Dakota (1889), art. 5, sec. 128; Constitution of South Dakota (1889), art. 7, sec. 9; Constitution of Idaho, art. 6, sec. 2, and Elections Law of Feb. 25, 1891, sec. 2; Public Acts of Michigan, 1881, No. 158 and No. 164, c. 2, sec. 17, c. 3, sec. 4 (Howell's General Statutes, 1882, secs. 781, 782, 5049. Women may not vote in city school elections; Mudge *v.* Stebbins, 59 Mich. 165); Minnesota Laws, 1876, c. 14, sec. 1, and 1885, c. 204 (Kelly's General Statutes, 1891, sec. 3302. Constitutionality upheld in State *v.* Gorton, 33 Minn. 345); Law of the Territory of Montana, March 8, 1883, and Constitution of the State of Montana (1889), art. 9, sec. 10; General Laws of New Hampshire (1878), c. 87, sec. 6, and c. 89, sec. 1; New Jersey Public Instruction Act (Revision), March 27, 1874, sec. 31, and Public Laws of 1887, c. 116; New York Laws, 1880, c. 9, sec. 1, and Public Instruction Law as amended June 15, 1886, Laws 1886, c. 655 (Throop's Revised Statutes, 1889, pp. 1288, 1329); Oregon Laws of Oct. 18, 1878, sec. 8, and Oct. 26, 1882, sec. 13 (Miscell. Laws, 1887, secs. 2609, 2637); Revised Laws of Vermont, secs. 524, 2659; Constitution of Washington, art. 7, sec. 2, and School Law of March 27, 1890, secs. 58, 78; Revised Statutes of Wisconsin (1878), c. 27, sec. 513, and Laws 1885, c. 211 (submitted to

the State of Wyoming, where women vote at all elections, and the State of Kansas, where they possess complete local suffrage. Lastly, Kentucky and Nebraska admit women only to the school franchise, and that only under special conditions.[1] As a general rule, the right to vote at the elections for school offices or to take part in the assemblies of the school district, depends on the obligation of paying taxes or the possession of the political franchise, besides the conditions of age and residence. The law of Nebraska admits to vote on school matters, all taxpayers of either sex, and, in addition, parents resident in the district who have children of school age, without reference to their property qualification. The law of Kentucky gives the vote, for all school matters, without any property qualification, to widows having children between the ages of six and twenty years; widows without children, and spinsters, who are absolutely excluded from the vote for the election of school trustees, are, if taxpayers, allowed to vote on the imposition of taxes in aid of the common schools.

§ 7.—The Delegation and Attribution of the Property Qualification.

(1) The right of a woman to transfer her property qualification to a man in order to establish or complete his

popular vote and carried November, 1886); Revised Statutes of Arizona (1887), sec. 1527.

[1] Common School Law of Kentucky, May 12 (1884), art. 3, sec. 2; art. 8, sec. 1; (Bullit and Feland, General Statutes, 1887, c. 96a); Compiled Statutes of Nebraska (Brown and Wheeler, 1889), c. 79, sub-div. 2, sec. 4, as amended by Laws 1883, c. 72, and 1889, c. 78.

qualification for a vote, which obtains in Italy at legislative elections, applies here to communal and provincial elections too. The widow or woman partially divorced from her husband can delegate her qualification to a son or a son-in-law whom she chooses.[1] Another country, which does not admit the transfer of property qualification for political elections, admits it for local elections. That is the rule in Roumania, where the widow or spinster of full age can delegate her qualification to her son-in-law, father or brother, and thus secure for one of them the communal franchise.[2]

(2) The attribution by right to the husband of the taxes paid by his wife obtains in the case of local elections in all countries where it is admitted for political elections, *viz.*, in Belgium,[3] Luxembourg,[4] Italy,[5] and Roumania.[6] In Luxembourg the taxes paid by women are attributed not only to the husband of the woman, but also to the eldest son of a widow, or, if she has none, to her eldest son-in-law.[7] In the Prussian towns, where women are excluded from the suffrage, their taxes, and generally all their property qualifications, which carry with them a vote, are accounted to the husband,[8] so as to give him a right to take part in the appointment of electors, who

[1] Article 21 of the Communal Law.

[2] Communal Law of 5th April, 1874, § 22.

[3] Electoral Code of 5th August, 1881, art. 14.

[4] Electoral Law of 5th March, 1884, art. 9.

[5] Article 19 of the Communal Law.

[6] Communal Law of 5th April, 1874, § 22.

[7] Article 10 of the Communal Law.

[8] Städteordnung for the six eastern provinces of the Prussian Monarchy of the 20th May, 1853, § 5. Städteordnung for the province of Westphalia, 14th March, 1856, § 5.

are to choose the members of the municipal council (and those of the *Landtag* as well).

(3) Thus, to sum up, we find that in the domain of local self-government women are admitted to the electoral franchise in England and her colonies, in Sweden, Iceland, Finland, and Russia; in the rural districts in Austria, Prussia, Saxony, and Brunswick; and, last, in three States of the American Union—Wyoming, Kansas and Michigan. Further, women enjoy the school franchise in Norway and in about fifteen States of the great American Republic. Eligibility to office is granted to them only in school administration (in England, Norway, in the Swedish capital, and in more than half of the States of the American Union), in poor-relief administration (in England, Sweden, and Finland), and as regards municipal offices generally, in Wyoming and Kansas. In Russia (except in the village assemblies), Austria, and Prussia, female electors can only vote by proxy, but everywhere else they have the power of voting in person.

CHAPTER IV.

Public Offices and Employments.

§ 1.—PUBLIC SERVICE.

(1) HAVING completed our examination of the part allotted to women in the government of the State, and of the secondary organs of the body politic, which constitute the domain of local self-government, we have now to pursue our inquiry into the following sphere, viz., that of the application of the law. The application of the law, which is the object of all administration, executive and judicial, is entrusted by the State to individuals, as a special commission, that is, as *public functions*.

Can women be invested with these public functions? The texts of the laws, with some few exceptions, which I shall presently point out, give no answer to this question. The precedents are neither many nor conclusive, for they happened under the sway of principles of public law, if one may so call them, which in the present times are repudiated generally. In England, for example, in the Middle Ages, and even down to our own times, we find examples of women who have occupied high offices in the State, as those of high constable, great chamberlain, champion at the coronation,[1] sheriff, clerk of the crown in the Court of

[1] The duties of champion consist in appearing on horseback at the coronation banquet of a new monarch, and challenging to single

King's Bench, etc.[1] But the characteristic of all these offices was that the performance of them could be delegated, and always was delegated[2] to persons of the male sex, so that women were only titular holders of these offices, and held them, as it were, in *nudum jus proprietatis*. In fact, most of these offices were hereditary, and came to women by right of property. But according to the principles of modern law, which no longer admit of such a confusion between private and public law, public offices are held in the interests of the State, not of the individual. And it is in the principles of public law that we must, in the absence of positive texts, seek for the answer to the question propounded.

(2) Assuming as granted, that the exercise of the highest public powers in the State is not a "right of man," but is subject to certain conditions, which limit the participation in the government to certain groups more or less numerous of the population, ought these powers to be delegated on different terms? Certainly not. The two things are correlative. Consequently women, who are not admitted to political power, ought not to be invested with duties which would allow them to manage the State mechanism.

But does that imply their absolute exclusion from

combat whoever doubts the rights of the king to the throne. If no one accepts the challenge, the champion mounted on his horse leaves the hall backwards.

[1] "Modern Reports," vii., 270.

[2] Though Anne, Countess of Pembroke, who inherited the office of Sheriff of Westmoreland, was anxious to fulfil the duties of the office herself (in the reign of James I.). See Law Reports, Court of Common Pleas, vol. iv., 1869, p. 390, etc., in the historical exposition given by Judge Willes.

every public office? Because a certain act has to do with State affairs, should persons who are not members of the body politic be forbidden to perform it? A distinction must be drawn. Every act or movement is made up of the idea which conceives it, the will which decides it, and the doings and reflex actions which execute it. In the organism of the State, this work is distributed among several organs, in a certain order which makes up the hierarchy of public services and public servants. Placed as they are on the different steps of the ladder, some of these servants take part in the conception and volition of the acts, of which the work of States is composed, whilst others are only the more or less unconscious instruments directed from above; though in the service of the State and employed by it, they have no share in public authority. The duties of the first class necessarily presuppose the possession of political rights, and are not, therefore, accessible to persons generally deprived of this right by reason of their sex, age, or nationality,[1] unless expressly authorised by law. In the absence of such a provision, the admission of women to the said offices would certainly be a breach of the established principles of public law. But, on the other hand, the tenure by women of offices or temporary employments in the public service, which are in no way offices of *government*, and which do not carry with them

[1] Among the reasons which entail exclusion from political rights, and, consequently, from public offices, I do not include the absence of a property qualification; for the absence of this legal presumption of political capacity is more than counterbalanced by the direct proof of capacity which public officers must furnish to be admitted to their offices.

imperium nor *jurisdictio*, do not hurt in any way the principles of public law.

Of the two branches of the public service, the administrative and the judicial, it is only within the first that we can trace a line of demarcation in the direction indicated above. In the judicial branch all the offices, from the top to the bottom of the ladder, are of the same character; they all form an immediate delegation of sovereignty; their holders, whatever their rank, are direct representatives of the majesty of the monarch or of the people, in whose name they dispense justice. Consequently no judicial office can be accessible to women except in the State of Wyoming.

The duties of the administrative branch do not possess this absolute character. They commence with the delicate task of laying down principles, of tracing the great lines to follow in the application of the laws, and end by the matter-of-fact execution, often mechanical, of prescribed rules. Assuming that the duties of the first rank are essentially those of *government*, of *imperium*, the other duties have clearly no connection with it, and can, consequently, be delegated to any person who combines the necessary qualifications of capacity and morality. In the absence of a formal prohibition of law, the appointment of women to posts of this sort will depend entirely on those who have to make the appointments, and who will be guided by the interests of the service and also by the prevailing public opinion, which no responsible administrator would openly offend.[1]

[1] Recently (February 26, 1891) in the House of Commons a question was addressed to the Secretary of State for the Home Department, whether he had the right to appoint women to the office of

For this sole reason it would be useless to attempt to draw a fixed line of demarcation between the offices which ought to be accessible to women and those from which they ought to be excluded. The current classifications of State servants as *authorities* and *employés*, or as *functionaries* and *government agents*, would certainly not facilitate the task, for the terms themselves are vague and arbitrary. It is according to the nature of the duty and the circumstances in which it ought to be performed, that the admissibility or exclusion of women must be determined, always bearing in mind the principle that I have laid down.

(3) That is the way in which the question has been solved in most countries for some time past. The statutory law did not contain any provisions as to the sex of persons admissible to public offices. The matter was implicitly disposed of in the Constitutions of several States of the American Union. They decided on the one hand that no one but electors of the State could be elected or appointed to public offices,[1] and on the other hand that the qualification of elector belonged to male persons only. But the posts to which the consti-

inspectors of factories and workshops, or whether it was necessary that these powers should be given him by law? The Secretary of State replied that such a law was not required, but that he did not think he ought to exercise his right to appoint women to those offices, "on the grounds of administration and practicability." However, the Home Secretary in the next Administration formed by Mr. Gladstone, has seen his way to appoint (in 1893) two ladies as factory inspectors.

[1] Cf. the Constitutions of Colorado, art. 7, sec. 6; Connecticut, art. 6., sec. 4; Indiana, art. 6, sec. 4; Louisiana, tit. vi., art. 105; Ohio, art. 15, sec. 4; Rhode Island, art. 9, sec. 1; West Virginia, art. 4, sec. 4; etc.

tutional texts made allusion were the superior offices mentioned with more or less preciseness in the Constitution itself. For the subordinate posts of the administrative branch, practice has established that women can be admitted to them, even in the absence of legislative provision. So they have been appointed not only in the States but also in the Federal public service to the postal department and to the central administrative departments at Washington; charged with the same duties as men, they are generally paid at a lower rate (the difference varies from a third to a half). Besides purely administrative posts, those connected with public education or school management are open to them, as I have already mentioned. School administration in the United States, being in nearly all its stages elective, and thus forming one of the objects of self-government, I thought it more convenient to speak of it in a former chapter devoted to local self-government. It may be added here, that from the superior posts, such for example as State Superintendent of Education, which is not always elective, women are excluded by law.

(4) In Europe the career of teacher in girls' schools was the first to be thrown open to women. This was soon extended to boys' primary schools, and partly also to the first forms of schools for intermediate education. Two or three countries have even furnished an example of women occupying professorial chairs.[1] On this point the Mediæval Italian age has many precedents, and

[1] At the University of Stockholm a Russian lady, lately deceased, was Professor of Mathematics, whilst another lady has recently been admitted to lecture on Jurisprudence in the University of Zurich in Switzerland. In Italy there is as well a lady lecturer at one of the Universities.

especially in the teaching of Jurisprudence. At the University of Bologna, some women have made themselves famous in the Chair of Jurisprudence, either as deputies of their fathers or husbands who were professors, or as professors themselves. Sometimes it so happened that the charm of their persons was no less powerful than the fascination of their juridical knowledge; as, for example, Novella Calderina (in the thirteenth century), who delivered her lectures enveloped in a thick veil, so that her striking beauty should not divert the attention of the undergraduates from the niceties of Roman law which she was expounding.[1]

Outside the sphere of public education, women have obtained access to subordinate situations in the postal, telegraph, and railway departments. They are admitted to these posts either by virtue of general rules established by ordinances or decrees or else by the tolerance of the administration, which admits women to the public service after having "dispensed them of their sex," as the bureaucratic phraseology of certain countries expresses it.

Statutory laws for the admission of women to the public service or their exclusion therefrom, do not exist, as I have already observed. Russia has a general regulation on the subject, passed in 1871, in the form of an Imperial order, sanctioning a resolution of the State ministers in council. This regulation prescribes, that outside the sphere of public education, "where their employment is to be encouraged and extended," women can be admitted to subordinate posts in the medical ser-

[1] Santoni de Sio, "La donna e l'avocatura," Rome. 1884. Part 1, p. 139.

vice, the telegraph offices, the bookkeeping service of the Education Department of higher schools and colleges for girls, as well as of those schools and colleges themselves; but that, with these exceptions, the admission of women into any public service, as clerks or in any other post, either filled up by Government appointment or by election, is forbidden.[1]

A general provision about the admissibility, or rather the non-admissibility, of women to the public service, is incidentally found in the Danish Royal ordinance of the 25th June, 1875, on admission of women to the University of Copenhagen. Article 3 of this decree provides that university examinations and academic degrees are not to give women access to administrative posts.[2]

In France women are admitted to the office of post-office managers (*receveuses*), prison inspectresses, school-mistresses, managers of infant schools, and some other subordinate posts in the State establishment.[3] In addition to this, by two recent laws, women have been introduced into the administration of public education, since it has been managed by councils which are partly elective. It is to these councils that women have been admitted by the law of the 27th February, 1880, relating to the Higher Council of Public Education, and by the law of the 30th October, 1886, on the organisation of primary education. In the *Département* (county) council of primary education there are three lady members, one

[1] Ordinance of the 14th January, 1871. (Complete Collection of Laws, 1871); No. 49137.

[2] "Annual Register," v. 301.

[3] Comp. Block, "Dictionnaire d'Administration," V° "Femmes."

the *directress* of the local Normal school of teachers, who is an *ex-officio* member, while the two other ladies are chosen by their colleagues, the female public teachers of the *Département* (Art. 44). Then there are female voters for the Higher Council: the directresses of the primary Normal schools, the inspectresses-general, and the special inspectresses of infant schools, take part in the election of six representatives for primary education, who sit at the Council (Art. 1 of the Law of 1880). Being in possession of the electoral vote, women are eligible as well for the Higher Council,[1] which has not only to deliberate upon matters of great importance to the State and society, but possesses also administrative powers of jurisdiction.[2]

§ 2.—Jury.

The system of employing free representatives of society in conjunction with State functionaries for the exercise in common of public duties, though relatively of recent origin in the administrative branch, is far more ancient in the judicial branch of the public service. Of the different forms that this representative system assumes in contemporary judicial procedure, the most general is that of a jury in criminal cases. Invested

1 There has been a lady elected to the Council, and she has sat there for several sessions.

2 The Higher Council gives judgment as a court of appeal and last resort against the decisions of the academic councils in contentious or disciplinary matters; it also gives judgment as a court of appeal and last resort against the decisions of the departmental councils, by which primary teachers, public or private, have been suspended for ever from teaching.

with a temporary commission to assist the permanent judges, jurors unite with them in dispensing justice, and like them share thereby in the exercise of public power. Consequently the question of the admissibility of women to a jury must receive the same answer that we have already found to the question of their appointment to the office of judge, unless there are special exceptions by law established. None of the codes in existence contain any such provision. For the most part they expressly require the enjoyment of political and civil rights or the qualification of an elector.[1] An explicit statutory provision as to the sex of the jurors is to be found, may be, in only one European country—the very country where the institution of trial by jury is of such ancient origin that it cannot be traced to any legislative enactment, that is, England. The law of the 9th August, 1870, whose short title is "The Juries Act, 1870," declares in one of its first provisions that the word juror shall mean male persons only.[2]

In America we find a similar provision in relation to the Territory of Utah, in the Act of Congress of the 23rd January, 1874, the fourth section of which provides, among other qualifications necessary for the office of juror, that of a male citizen.[3] Nevertheless, women have for some time served on juries in the United States,

[1] Comp. Art. 38 of the French Code of Criminal Procedure; the Law of 28th May, 1873, on the jury in Austria (Art. 1); the Italian Law of 8th June, 1874 (Art. 2); Art. 81 and 82 of the Russian Judicial Organisation.

[2] 33 and 34 Vict., c. 71, sec. 5.

[3] An Act of Congress in relation to court and judicial officers in the Territory of Utah. (The Compiled Laws of Utah, 1876, p. 55.)

in the Territories of Wyoming and Washington. In Wyoming the judges appointed for the Territory, at the time of its formation (by the President of the United States), happened to be great partisans of women's rights. After the adoption of the law of Female Suffrage, they caused women to be empannelled as jurors. An express provision of law to make women admissible was rendered unnecessary, in the opinion of the judges, by the law of 1869, which confers on women the right to vote at elections and to *fill offices*. But this interpretation has since been declared unconstitutional, and women have ceased to serve on juries, after having sat for several sessions of assize, and furnished one subject more for the malignity of the public. [1]

In the Territory of Washington, women also sat on juries for some years by virtue of the law of 1883, which gave them the suffrage, the qualification for elector and juror being identical. But in 1887 this law was repealed by the Supreme Court of the Territory in the circumstances referred to above, namely in consequence of an appeal made by a person convicted in a court of assize after a trial where women had sat on the jury. This event put an end to women sitting on juries in the United States.

§ 3.—Court Officers, Notaries, etc.

Besides the judges who dispense justice, there are in the law courts, or in connection with them, officers

[1] From this time dates the couplet which had such great success:

"Baby, baby, don't get in a fury,
Your mother's gone to sit on the jury."

whose duty it is to assist the judges, and, when called upon by the parties, to perform for them certain legal ministrations provided by law. Whether salaried by the State like the clerks, or as private practitioners, like notaries and others, they hold their offices directly or indirectly from the chief of the State, and, consequently, admission to these posts is determined by the general regulations for admissibility to public employments.

In France these offices are described by the generic name of *offices ministériels*, and the most complete set of regulations on them which exists in the French legislation is that relating to notaries, an office which is, in other countries too, the principal, if not the only, "office of practice." The law concerning the Notariat, of 25th Ventôse of the 11th year (Republican era), excludes women from the duties of notary, by providing that admission can be obtained only by those who enjoy the exercise of the right of citizen, and have satisfied the law as to military conscription, etc. In other European countries, women find themselves excluded from the post of notary by virtue of the general principles as to admissibility to public employments.

In the United States the provisions on this matter vary in different States; sometimes they require that the candidate shall be a citizen of the United States, as in Illinois[1]; sometimes an elector, as in Minnesota[2]; sometimes, as in Massachusetts, they require that notaries shall be appointed on the same conditions as public officials[3]; sometimes, and more frequently, they content

[1] Revised Statutes (Ed. 1881), ch. 90, sec. 1.
[2] The General Statutes (1881), p. 319.
[3] Statutes, p. 38.

themselves with a general indication that the "governor of the State shall appoint to the office of notary as many persons as he shall think necessary." Attempts made by females to gain access to the post of notary through the governors have been rejected in some States and have met with success in others. Lastly, two States, Ohio and Wisconsin, have passed special laws for admitting women to the office of notary public.[1]

§ 4.—The Bar.

(1) The number of functions clothed with a public character is not exhausted with the hierarchy of the State service (administrative and judicial branches) and the offices of court officers, notaries, etc. There is, in addition, attached to the judicial order an organisation, which, on the other hand, by many of its lines, runs into the free professions. I mean the institution of the Bar. Is it so bound up with the administration of justice that the question of the admissibility of women to the Bar must be decided in accordance with the principles of public law, or, on the contrary, is the connection rather mechanical than constitutional, so as to preserve the complete independence of the Bar as a private profession?

This problem has not attracted the attention of the legislator, but in recent years it has come to the front in practice in different countries of Europe and America. The question raised was whether a woman may be an advocate. The traditions of the Roman law were not in

[1] The Revised Statutes of Ohio (Ed. 1879), sec. 110.
Supplement to the Revised Statutes of Wisconsin (Ed. 1883), chap. xiii., sec. 173.

favour of women. At Rome they were at first admitted to the Forum, but their intemperance of language, and especially the scandalous conduct of a certain Cafrania brought on them an express prohibition from appearing as attorneys. The Law I., § 5, Dig. III., 1 (de postulando), provides: "Prætor excepit sexum, dum feminas prohibet pro aliis postulare; et ratio quidem prohibendi, ne contra pudicitatem sexui congruentem alienis causis se immisceant, ne virilibus officiis fungantur mulieres. Origo vero introducta est a Cafrania improbissima femina quæ invercunde postulans et magistratum inquietans causam dedit edicto." [1] Whilst the Theodosian Code allowed women to plead their own causes (de postulando II., 10), the legislation of Justinian absolutely forbade them to appear in a court of justice, as shown by this general rule enacted with regard to them: "Feminæ ab omnibus officiis civilibus vel publicis remotæ sunt, et ideo nec judices esse possunt, nec magistratum gerere, nec postulare, nec pro aliis intervenire, nec procuratores existere" (2 Dig. II., 17).[2] The customary law of the Middle Ages endorsed the precepts of the Roman law, whilst recalling the circumstances in which they had been adopted. So, *e.g.*, the "Mirror of Swabia"

[1] "The Praetor has excluded the sex, as he prohibits women from interceding on behalf of others; and this prohibition is for the reason that females should not, in defiance of the modesty becoming to their sex, meddle with strangers' business, and that women should not perform the functions of men. That comes from a wretched woman Cafrania, who by her impudent pleading and worrying the magistrate caused this edict to be enacted."

[2] "Women are excluded from all offices, whether civil or public, and therefore cannot be judges, fill any magistracy, appear in court, intercede on others behalf, or receive powers of attorney."

declares that: "Nulle fame ne puet estre tuerriz de soi meimes, ne porter la parole en justice, ne lautrui, ne complaindre dautrui sans avocat. Ce hunt elles perdu par un gentil dame qui fu de Rome qui ot non Caefurna, qui ot a Rome, per devant le roi si foles contenances."[1] Beaumanoir again states in the "Coutumes de Beauvoisis": "Il ne loist pas a feme a estre en office d'avocat por autrui por loier; mais sans loier pot ele parler por li ou por ses enfans ou por aucun de son lignage, mais que ce soit de l'auctorité de son baron se ele a baron."[2]

The social position which women occupied till lately, as well as the organisation of judicial procedure, did not allow any departure from this rule. With difficulty we can find examples of women who have been permitted to plead their own cause. The case of the Marquise of Créqui may be quoted, who was allowed to plead before the Parliament of Paris. In 1807, a similar favour was granted by the Court of Cassation to Mlle. Legracieux de Lacoste. When the movement for the emancipation of women, started in our time, and the modern necessities of the struggle for life, aroused in

[1] "No woman can by herself assume guardianship, or plead in court, or sue without an advocate. They disgraced themselves by a gentle dame who was from Rome, and whose name was Caefurna, who behaved herself so foolishly before the king." (The "Mirror of Swabia," according to the French manuscript of the town library of Berne, published by G. A. Mathile, Neufchâtel (1843), pp. 43, 44.)

[2] "A woman is not allowed to be an advocate to advise others; she may, however, without advising, plead for herself, for her children, or for some of her kin, but only with the authority of her husband if she has still one." "Coutumes de Beauvoisis," edit. Beugnot., P., 1852, I., chap. v. (Advocates) p. 95, § 16.

women the desire to enter upon the different careers which had formerly been closed to them by law and still more by custom, they turned their attention also to the career of the Bar. America set the ball rolling. It rebounded on Europe in a slight degree only, in the form of individual claims in a few isolated cases, and they were speedily rejected. The law courts had to pronounce on the admissibility of women to the office of advocate in Italy, Belgium, Switzerland, and Russia. It was especially in the two first countries that the question came up for discussion in the terms I stated at the beginning of this section. An examination of the cases which came before the Italian and Belgian courts may therefore furnish us with material for the solution of the problem.

(2) In 1883, Signorina Lydia Poët, Doctor of Law, graduated at the University of Turin, claimed to be admitted to the Bar of that city. The Benchers admitted her by a majority of votes. The Procureur-General (State Attorney) intervening, by the right conferred upon him by his office, reported the Benchers' decision to the Court of Appeal, which annulled it. Signorina Poët appealed to the Supreme Court, but this tribunal too set aside her contention and confirmed the judgment of the Lower Court. According to the judgment of the High Court, the profession of advocate could not be compared to any other profession, for the exercise of which it was sufficient to have completed a course of studies and obtained a diploma; the functions of advocate were something more than a profession; it was a kind of public and necessary office, and whilst those who exercise other professions are free to give or withhold the service

claimed of them, advocates could not refuse to appear, especially in cases where they are appointed by the magistrate. Treating them as auxiliaries of justice, the Italian law has organised them in colleges, with a legal representation, and has given them special rights to be raised to the magistracy, to be appointed praetors, judges, councillors of appeal, and of the Supreme Court, after they have exercised the profession of advocate for a certain period. If women were admitted to the Bar, they could also exercise these judicial functions, but such was certainly not the intention of the legislator. The profession of advocate being thus a public office, or, at all events, a quasi-public office, it is not sufficient, in order that women should be admitted to it, to say that in the law for the time being there is no express provision to exclude them. It would require a formal text declaring women capable of holding all offices and employments, both public and civil.[1]

(3) Some years later (in 1888), a similar case occurred in Belgium. Mlle. Popelin, licentiate of law, appeared before the Court at Brussels claiming to be sworn in as advocate. The Procureur-General was of opinion that she could not be admitted. The arguments which he brought forward may be summed up thus:—If a woman wishes to be admitted to the Bar, it requires a new and special law. Napoleon's decree[2] of 1810 on the organisa-

[1] The complete report of the judgment of the Court of Appeal and the Supreme Court of Turin, is to be found in the work of M. Santoni de Sio, "La donna e l'avocatura. Studio guiridico-soci ale," I., pp. 8-26. Rome. 1884.

[2] Belgium was then part of French territory, and several portions of Napoleonic legislation have remained in force there to the present day.

tion of the Bar is silent on the subject; but the spirit of the decree is sufficiently known. Napoleon's opinions about advocates as a "set of babblers" are known enough to enable us to affirm with certainty that at no price would he have admitted women, whom he loved still less. He would have been a bold man who had proposed such a thing. Then the Procureur-General referred to precedents, and argued that the Digest, more than 1200 years old, closed the Bar to females, and that from the time that codified laws succeeded primitive regulations and usages, the practice of the profession of advocate was forbidden to women. Passing on to the discussions and labours from which the present legislation has resulted, the Procureur cited several extracts, all proving, in his opinion, beyond dispute, the intent of reserving for men only the profession of advocate. "It is especially desirable to train *men* capable of appreciating the merit of the laws and of making a just application thereof"; "it is necessary to train distinguished *men* for the office of advocate." Is not, argued the Procureur-General, the bringing together of these expressions with the word civil office convincing? To say that *man* means human being of whatever sex would not be accurate. When the law does not intend to make any distinction between the sexes, the term it makes use of is *every person.* The Procureur further argued that the advocate, without being a public official in the administrative sense, since he has not the investiture conferred on him by Government, does exercise a judicial function. He collaborates in the dispensing of justice, as is shown by the fact that if there are not occasionally judges enough to hear cases, the advocates present in Court are called upon to sit on the Bench. Thence it follows that a woman can only be an advocate if she is capable of filling the office of judge. And no one maintains that a woman can be a judge. If it is said that the diploma alone is sufficient to give the right of being admitted to the Bar, what becomes of the political oath which the advocate has to take, the Benchers' disciplinary power, the probationary period? In conclusion, the Procureur-General declared, that in the present state of legislation and opinion, women could neither hold the title nor exercise the profession of advocate, and that on the day when they were admitted to the Bar there would be an end to the independence and dignity of the Bar. The Court adopted his conclusions, and declined to admit Mlle. Popelin to take the oath of advocate.[1]

The arguments presented to the Court by the two Counsels for the claimant were based on moral considerations[2] and juridical principles. The legal arguments brought forward by the junior counsel (and already published by him in a pamphlet[3] somewhile before the hearing of the case), went to establish that "no reason could be found either in social science or in the spirit of

[1] See the report of the case in the "Indépendance Belge" of the 4th and 13th December, 1888.

[2] The senior counsel for Mlle. Popelin, late chairman of the Benchers, and one of the leaders of the Belgian Bar, expressed himself thus:—"What we ask for is that you should proclaim the equality of woman; we ask it in the name of Christianity, which, rising up as a protest against Roman corruption and infamy, restored her rights and her liberties to woman—mother, sister, and wife—all that we cherish, all that we venerate here below since our eyes first saw the light of day." (*Ibid*).

[3] "La femme avocat," by L. Frank. Brussels, 1888.

private law for excluding women from the Bar. We have not, urged M. Frank, to concern ourselves with the spirit of public law, seeing that the enjoyment of political rights is not one of the qualifications for the exercise of the profession of advocate. The legal capacity of women is a fundamental rule of our legislation. Whenever restraint is placed on this capacity, the Code takes care to declare the restriction in a formal provision. Articles 37, 442, and 980 prove this. Save the cases of incapacity, which are expressly stated, the Code has established the principle of woman's capacity. Were it otherwise, Article 8 of the Civil Code, which declares that every French subject without distinction of sex enjoys civil rights, would have no meaning. It has been contended that the profession of advocate is a public office. If the advocate was a judicial officer, he would hold from the Government his office, and any insult addressed to him in the performance of his duties would be punished with the special penalties for the outrage of public officers, but it is not so. Besides, even were the office of advocate regarded as a public office, women would still have the right to hold it, seeing that no provision, constitutional or legal, excludes women from public offices. On the contrary, the Constitution declares all Belgians admissible to civil employment, reserving exceptions, which may be established by a law for particular cases. Supposing that the profession of advocate was a public office, a special law would be necessary to establish the woman's incapacity to hold that office. The argument drawn from Article 203 of the Judicial Ordinance, which allows an advocate to be called on to take the place of a judge at the tribunal, is nullified by the fact that advocates of foreign nationality are admitted to the Bar, but are not allowed to be called on to sit at the Bench.[1] As to the diploma, it has been recognised that although it may be called in question with regard to admission to an office, it is beyond discussion as to the right which it confers to practise a profession. Lastly, if the intention of the framers of the decree of 1810 had been to exclude women from the Bar, they ought to have declared their intention in formal language, as was done with regard to the Notariat by the law of 25th Ventôse of the year 11 (Republican era), which provided that to be admitted to the office of notary it was necessary (1) to enjoy the exercise of the rights of citizen; (2) to have satisfied the laws of military conscription, etc. Now, there is an opinion generally adopted in matters of interpretation, that where the law is silent, judges are bound to admit the claimant's plea, if it seems to them to be in accord with natural equity. No one would contend, said M. Frank, in conclusion, that the claim of Mlle. Popelin was not in accord with natural equity."

(4) If the principles of interpretation of public law, which have served as our guide throughout this inquiry, are correct, then the reasons advanced for the admission of women to the Bar, notwithstanding the absence of an express legal authorisation, are over-ruled. The arguments drawn from the spirit of private law and from the civil capacity of women, and still more from social science and Christianity, are outside the real point at issue, which consists in ascertaining whether the office of

[1] The Procureur-General in his turn met this argument by referring to French Jurisprudence, which refused a stranger admission to the Bar.

advocate is or is not clothed with a public character. The only considerations presented from this last point of view, in favour of the woman advocate, consist in the argument that the advocate is not invested with his functions by the Government, and does not enjoy the special privilege of the public officer against injuries which he receives in the performance of his duties.

But these reasons are inconclusive to show that the post of advocate is not of a public character. Instead of grappling with the question, they only touch one side of it, that of the personal position of the advocate from the point of view of administrative organisation. Confounding *officialism* with *office,* and finding that the advocate does not fulfil the conditions of officialism, it has been hastily concluded that the post of advocate was not of a public character. To determine its character we must, above all, examine the nature of the duties. And that is defined from the ancient times by the rule of the Prætor, "Si non habebunt advocatum ego dabo" (if they have no advocate I will give them one), so necessary was considered the intervention of an advocate in the administration of justice. In modern society the progress of civilisation manifests itself in the administration of justice by the constant extension of the part of the defence, so that the function of advocate becomes an integral part of the judicial organism, and works regularly in every stage of the trial from the beginning to the end. In fact, it is in this way only that the strict play of the see-saw of justice is secured. If one of the ends has nothing to counter-balance it and falls back with all its weight, it is the entire frame of society which is shaken in the person of the injured suitor. The possibility alone of a similar mishap is a menace against society, a danger which it exposes itself to before it has arisen. The office of advocate, associated with justice, in order to avert these perils from society, is, therefore, a public office.

The objection raised that the duties of advocate are not obligatory like those of public officers is ineffectual. It is again to apply the argument to the person who may fill the office, and not to the office itself. The duty of advocate is not compulsory in so far as it concerns this or that leader of the Bar; the advocate can choose his client as the client can choose his advocate, but there will always have to be an advocate to plead the case, "si non habebunt advocatum ego dabo"; where the accused cannot find someone to defend him, the codes declare generally (*Cf.* French Code of Criminal Procedure, Art. 294, and several other codes) that one will be officially appointed, or the proceedings will be invalid. If public officers working for clients, such as notaries, registrars, etc., cannot refuse their services, it is because the nature of the acts which they are called on to perform is determined beforehand by set rules, whilst the advocate is supposed, in each particular case, to have his conscience and the claims which he supports before the tribunal in complete harmony. In order that this harmony, so indispensable to the administration of justice, should be secured, it is necessary to give the advocate liberty to form his convictions. So that the liberty of the advocate, which, from the point of view of officialism, constitutes the private character of the profession, is in reality only the first condition of the exercise by the advocate of his public mission. "Without the precious right of granting or refusing their services, advocates would soon cease to inspire confidence," . . . "the Court would be always condemned to doubt their good faith," and "an empty phantom of justice would take the place of that beneficent authority."[1]

If at the same time the reciprocal freedom of choice between advocate and client communicates to the agency of the advocate the character of a profession, that is only part of the situation; it is not the whole situation. The professional element not only does not absorb the public character of the office, but it is plainly subordinate to it. The preliminary negotiations which have brought to the Bar for this or that case leader A and not leader B are quite immaterial to law and justice. The private transaction, which precedes the judicial proceedings, dies away, so to speak, at the threshold of the tribunal. Within the precincts of the Court there are only persons charged one and all with the duty of collaborating in the administration of justice, with all the public responsibility which attaches to such a duty. In accordance with the unwritten law which rules the Bar in France, the agreement between advocate and client has so little to do with the appearance of the advocate in Court, that in cases where he, using the right of a contracting party in a private transaction, sues for the recovery of his fees, he is liable to be struck off the rolls of the Bar. For, in the cause of the individual, he is considered to have served another cause, *viz.*, that of justice and society, and to have fulfilled a public duty

[1] Report to the King, of 20th November, 1822, by the Keeper of the Seals, M. de Peyronnet, relating to the ordinance of the same date on the organisation of the Bar in France.

which is not dependent on wages paid by an individual. If practice tends to swerve from these principles, if sometimes the office of advocate is worked like a commercial business, does that reverse the nature and the object of the office ? Does it not rather follow that men should rise to their duties and not that the duties should be lowered to the weaknesses of men ?

The fact that the advocate has not all the qualifications of an "official" does not in the least affect the intrinsic nature of his office. That it is perfectly possible to fill a public office without being an "official," we have already seen in the case of jurors, who are not even "received by our Courts" (as the French Royal Ordinance relating to advocates puts it), but selected by the chance drawing of lots, and after having accomplished their temporary duty return to the body of the people. All the conditions mentioned, the absence of which, in the case of advocates, are said to deprive this office of a public character (the mode of investiture, the special protection given to officials to enhance their dignity), are really external qualifications only, which point above all to the personal position and the hierarchic relations of the official with the authorities, rather than show the connection with the general interests of society.

In the matter of the liberty of the profession of advocate, so often loudly asserted in the name of the Bar itself, the question was frequently regarded from the point of view of the advocate's position towards the authorities, and on such occasion stress was laid on the private character of the profession: "The advocate is really only a private citizen who devotes himself to the defence of others;" "Advocates have no personality distinguished from their private personality;" "The advocate has never been a public official;" "His duties do not imply any privilege or concession of power;" "He is not specially bound except to obey his conscience—a discipline he imposes on himself;" "A citizen is not an advocate because the Government has consented to give him a commission;" "The advocate neither hopes nor fears anything from a superior;" "He certainly owes respect to the judges, but is he, therefore, to be held in real *subjection* or in a particular dependence?"[1] etc. The anxiety which these sayings disclose is legitimate. But to vindicate *this* independence, is it necessary to screen themselves behind the fence of a private house, and at the approach of every assailant to cry out that their house is their castle? To the great or petty tyrants who would like, as Napoleon wrote, "to cut out the tongue of an advocate who uses it against the Government," could they not repeat the words in which the Cortes of Aragon were in the habit of addressing the new king on his accession: "*We who are as good as you*," and say: "We, too, hold a mission from society, in its name and in its interest do we fulfil it."

To sum up, the post of advocate, although it is not a public "office," is clothed with a public character, and is a public duty. Consequently, women, who are, rightly or wrongly, excluded from public life, can not be admitted to the Bar as a matter of right.

(5) In Switzerland the question of the admissibility

[1] I borrow these quotations from Carré, who in his chapter on advocates (Traité de l'organis. judic.,) sums up all the arguments on the question.

of women to exercise the profession of advocate was raised under the following circumstances. At Zurich, where there is no organised Bar, Madame K., Doctor-of-Law, appeared before the tribunal to plead a cause, but was not allowed to do so because of Article 174 of the Code of Procedure, which requires that persons representing third parties before the tribunals must be in possession of the "rights of an active citizen." Madame K. appealed to the Federal Tribunal. She based her appeal on the ground that the Cantonal Tribunal of Zurich, in preventing her from exercising her profession, had violated the fourth Article of the Federal Constitution, which declared that there was in Switzerland no privilege of place, or birth, or of (particular) families, or persons. The Federal Court were of opinion that the question was as to the interpretation of a Cantonal law, which it was not within their competency to decide, that the Federal Constitution had no provision in it enabling them to say in what sense the right of an active citizen carried with it the power of representing third parties before the tribunals, and that besides, taking, as they must, that the right of an active citizen is equivalent in Zurich to the right of franchise, there was no violation of the Constitution, as the franchise belonged to men only and not to women.[1]

(6) Russia was the first country, in chronological order, in which the question of women advocates was brought before the tribunals; it is true that it was not with respect to advocates of the Bar. Prior to 1874, there was in Russia absolute liberty as regards the profession of

[1] "Entscheidungen des Schweitzerischen Bundesgerichts," (1887) vol. xiii., p. 1.

advocate: every person, armed with a power of attorney, could plead for his principal before any judicial court. The Bar possessed only the moral superiority of learning and character. Under cover of this liberty there sprang up a class of law agents of low standing, who were far from furnishing the necessary guarantees of capacity and morality. Then came the law of the 25th May, 1874, with the rule that besides the "sworn advocates" of the Bar, no one could practise except persons who, after having been examined by the tribunals, had obtained a certificate of "private attorney," renewable each year and subject to a fee. Before 1874, there were women who appeared as attorneys and even pleaded. Some of these claimed to be admitted as "private attorneys," and were so admitted by several tribunals (of justices of the peace). The Minister of Justice having referred these decisions of the tribunals to the Court of Cassation, it decided that the law relating to private attorneys did not contain any restrictions as regards sex. The Minister appealed to the Emperor, who settled the question, by signing an Imperial order (of the 9th January, 1876) to the effect that the ordinance of 21st January, 1871, prohibiting the admission of women to the public service, applied equally to the office of advocate. This Imperial order was afterwards incorporated in the Judicature Code in the following terms: "Women cannot obtain certificate of private attorneys in judicial affairs" (Art. 406^{19}).

The question, so far as it affects the Bar, could not arise in Russia any more than in other countries where women are not allowed to attend the courses of professorial lectures and obtain the diplomas required for admission to the Bar. In Denmark a Royal decree of the 12th May, 1882, authorised women to present themselves for certain examinations in law, but took care to stipulate that they should not thereby obtain the right to practise as advocates, or to present themselves before the tribunals as agents of advocates, acting under power of attorney.

(7) In the United States the fate of the question of women advocates has been different from that in Europe. In certain States of the American Union the conditions of admissibility to practise as advocate (attorney, counsellor) were not regulated by the written law; in others the laws contained provisions similar to those already analysed with regard to officials and public notaries, that is to say, they require the qualification of "a citizen," or "an elector," or "a male person." From 1869, the claims of women to be admitted to take the oath of advocate have been repeatedly laid before the Courts. In several cases these demands were favourably received, and in a dozen States women obtained entry to the Bar, although they were not expressly authorised by law. It was in the lower tribunals especially that they were admitted; the higher Courts were much more reluctant to admit them. As they were only allowed to practise in the Court which gave them the permission, the consequence was that in the large towns, divided into several judicial districts, women were admitted for one district and rejected in another. The attempts which they made to break into the Bar, by virtue of Amendment XIV. of the Federal Constitution, were not more successful than when they tried to obtain by the same means a vote at elections. One lady, who was refused admission to the Bar by the Supreme

Court of Illinois, appealed to the Federal Court, basing her appeal on the primary right of everybody, man or woman, to choose his or her vocation for a livelihood. The Supreme Court of the United States decided that the practice of an advocate's profession was not one of the "privileges or immunities" which the legislation of a State can not abridge, and that the power of each State to lay down conditions for admission to the Bar was in no way prejudiced by Amendment XIV. of the Federal Constitution.[1] In the more rudimentary States of the West women continued to be readily admitted to the Bar.[2]

But in most of the States of New England the

[1] Decision of December, 1872, in the case of Bradwell *v.* The State (Wallace, "Cases in the Supreme Court," vol. xvi., p. 131, etc.).

[2] At Utah, for example, a woman was admitted to the Bar under these circumstances: The claim was presented to the Court by an advocate, who said, "I know, sir, that for the last three years, she [Miss Georgie Snow, daughter of the Attorney-General for the Territory] has been a devoted student in her father's office, in striving to obtain an understanding of the principles and practice of the law; but she has not dared to come forward to ask admission to the Bar. From my own examination I am enabled to state that she is fully competent to be admitted to this Bar; fully competent to meet almost any of us, not only in talking, but in reasoning at the Bar. And on this statement of my personal knowledge and examination, united with that of her father, as to her qualifications, I rise with pleasure to move her admission to the Bar, as the first of Utah's daughters who has entered the profession of the law." (Applause.) *Court*—"I am very happy to hear the remarks and motion of Major Hempstead. I have a personal acquaintance with Miss Snow, and I have no doubt of the correctness of the statement made in regard to her. Let me say here, however, that whatever may be the feeling of the members of the Bar on this subject, the Court must not

Law Courts resisted, until the legislature intervened in favour of women. Special laws authorising them to practise as advocates were adopted in the following States: California, Illinois, Iowa, Massachusetts, Minnesota, New York, Ohio and Wisconsin. The terms in which they set forth the right of women to practise as advocates are sometimes expressed, sometimes implied

take such a course as to render it liable to the charge of great partiality to the ladies. The major, in his enthusiasm, seems to have forgotten that our practice here is to require of gentlemen who have never been admitted to the Bar elsewhere, first to go before a committee of examination. Now, while this is a matter of form merely, and, of course, is so in this case, yet if I were to admit a lady, who has never been admitted to any other Bar, without referring her case to a committee, some young incompetent gentleman might apply here and plead that as a precedent in his case, and so place the Court in the embarrassing position of appearing to have one rule for one sex and another rule for the other sex. I think I will grant the motion in a modified form, or rather first appoint a committee and let them report. I will appoint as that committee Major Hempstead and W. Hodge. I have done that with several young gentlemen who have applied for admission, and taking that course in their case, will make it conform to the rule." Miss Snow being in Court, Messrs. Hempstead and Hodge retired and made the following report: "The application of Miss C. Georgie Snow for admission to the Bar of the Third Judicial District Court of Utah, having been by the Court referred to the undersigned for examination and to report thereon, the undersigned beg leave respectfully to report, that we have made a proper and necessary examination as to the qualifications of the said applicant, that she is an estimable lady, and by a long course of arduous study of the law is fully qualified for admission to the Bar. The undersigned therefore respectfully recommend the admission of Miss Snow to the Bar of the Court." The Court approved the report, and after Miss S. was sworn in, the members of the Bar were introduced to their new colleague.—(*Englishwoman's Review* of 1873, p. 18.)

The laws of California and Illinois proclaim, as a general rule, that no person shall on account of sex be disqualified from entering or pursuing any lawful business, vocation, or profession.[1] The laws of Iowa and Minnesota provide that *every person* shall be admitted to practise in the profession of attorney on condition, etc.[2] The laws of Massachusetts, New York, Ohio and Wisconsin stipulate expressly for the admission of women to the Bar.[3]

Lastly, a federal law has given women access to the Bar of the Supreme Court of the United States. By virtue of this important measure, adopted on the 15th February, 1879, any woman who shall have been for the space of three years a member of the Bar of the highest Court of any State or Territory, or of the Supreme Court of the District of Columbia, and shall have maintained a good standing before such Court, and who shall be a person of good moral character, shall, on motion, and the production of such record, be admitted to practise before the Supreme Court of the United States.[4]

[1] Constitution of California, art 20., sec. 18; Revised Statutes of Illinois (Chicago, 1881, by G. W. Cothram), c. 18, sec. 3.

[2] "New Revised and Annotated Code of Iowa" (by W. E. Miller, Des Moine, 1882), c. 9, sec. 208; The General Statutes of Minnesota (1881) c. 88, sec. 1.

[3] Acts and Resolves passed by the General Court of Massachusetts, 1882, Law of 10th April, 1882; Laws of the State of New York, 1886 (Law of 19th May, 1886, modifying paragraph 56 of the Code of Civil Procedure); The Revised Statutes of Ohio (Columbus, 1879), sec. 565; The Revised Statutes of Wisconsin (Madison, 1878), c. 117, sec. 2586, 5°.

[4] An Act to relieve certain legal disabilities of women ("Supplement to the Revised Statutes of the United States," vol i., p. 410. Wash., 1881).

It is with the examination of the question of women advocates that I intend to close this chapter, which is devoted to public duties and offices. Other professions than that of advocate need not be considered here, for they are not of a public character, and such a character could not, certainly, be given even to those of them which the State, in the fulness of its police jurisdiction, thinks fit to regulate. Doctors, chemists, druggists, dentists, architects, etc., unless they are in the State service, or charged by it with a special mission, do not take any part whatever in the exercise of public authority, and are not even indirectly connected with it. The public utility of their professions may be more or less important, but the exercise of them has no effect on the legal working of the public order. Whether individuals have recourse or not to the art of the dentist or the druggist, is the affair of the patients and the practitioners who can relieve their sufferings. If the right of these men to offer their services to the public is subject to certain restrictions for the general good, these restrictions affect their legal position only from the point of view of the liberty of the profession. Whether sex is or is not among the limitations imposed on the liberty of professions, is a question which will have to be examined hereafter when we come to consider the position of women from the point of view of the exercise of individual public rights, among which is included the liberty of professions.

CHAPTER V.

Individual Public Rights.

§ 1.—General Observations.

The public rights which have been the object of our enquiry in the preceding chapters do not spring up with the individual, nor do they exist for him as an individual. Derived not from his nature, but from the nature of society, they are exercised on behalf of society in the interests of the collective body, of the πολιτέια, whence comes their name of *political* rights. The benefit of these rights accrues only indirectly to the individual, who enjoys them as a citizen of the State. But though living on this reflected light, the individual as a man has light and warmth of his own; he has rights which are a part of his existence, and which since the latter end of the eighteenth century have been more than once proclaimed to the world as anterior to and superior to positive rights. Such are individual liberty, inviolability of the home, liberty of conscience, liberty of the press, right of meeting and of association, right of petition, etc. In France all the constitutions that have existed up to the time of the second empire, endorsed and sanctioned these principles under the name of "public rights of Frenchmen." However, in social economy these individual rights, called natural rights, are subject to more or less extensive limitations for the general interest. From that very cause they fall within the juridical domain, and consequently within the sphere of our present investigation. The enjoyment of these rights being wedded to positive law solely by the sacrifices imposed on the individual in their exercise, our attention may be confined to the restrictions introduced by the legislator. We must see, therefore, if there are any which relate to sex. Where no provision is found to exclude women from this or that public individual right, we shall have to acknowledge that it belongs to them, whilst with regard to political rights derived from society, it is on the contrary the express authority of the law that establishes the capacity of woman.

To determine the scope of our researches, let us remember that individual rights, called *natural* rights, present themselves in a double aspect. Some, as individual liberty, inviolability of the home, liberty of conscience, belong to the internal life of man, and demand from society no other favour than that which Diogenes asked of Alexander. These are *human* rights *par excellence,* which allow no distinction of age, sex, or nationality. We need not, therefore, occupy ourselves with them. Very different are the rights of meeting and of association, the liberty of the press, and the right of petition. Through these the individual aims at coming out of his person, at acting on the collective body, reacting on the public authorities, and even at laying hold of the management of the State. That is the reason why the State has often thought it its duty to take some precautions against encroachment by regulating the exercise of individual rights of a public character. It is in this direction that our researches will be prosecuted.

§ 2.—Right of Petition.

(1) The right of presenting petitions to the supreme authority, a right which, in its general sense, is admitted even in absolute monarchies, consists in the power of the citizen, who is injured in his rights and interests, and who has exhausted the ordinary legal means of defence, to have recourse to the justice and benevolence of the holders of the supreme power. In free countries, where the interests of the citizen are not limited to his personal concerns, but are also extended to public affairs, recourse to the King or Parliament is in its turn extended to collective grievances and demands of a general character. Answering thus two distinct purposes, the right of petition has practically become indivisible since it was raised to the rank of a *social guarantee* by English Constitutionalism and the French Revolution. All who possess it for the redress of personal grievances, as an extraordinary resource, can also make use of it for the expression of political demands and proposals.[1] The

[1] "By means of petition," says de Cormenin, the eminent lawyer and celebrated pamphleteer, "the last of the proletarians mounts the tribune and speaks publicly before the whole of France. By it the Frenchman, who is not eligible, nor an elector, nor even a citizen, can exercise the legislative initiative like Deputies, or like the Government itself" ("Droit Administratif." Paris, 1840, t. ii., p. 395). On influencing by petitions the legislative work of Parliament, see Lord Brougham's speech in Hansard, 1816, vol. cxxviii., p. 798.

Constitutions, nearly all of which sanction the right of petition, grant it, so to say, *en bloc,* and make no more distinction between the persons to whom this right is to belong than between the matters to which it is to relate. Constitutional practice has left no doubt whatever as to the power of women to use the right of political petition. In England they frequently used it before our time. At the great democratic outburst in the seventeenth century, we find the women of London petitioning the Long Parliament in 1643.[1] The first half of the present century was marked in England by great political agitations,

[1] Petition for peace presented to the House of Commons on the 9th of August, 1643, by the women of London. "The humble petition of many civilly-disposed Women inhabiting the cities of London, Westminster, the Suburbs and Parts adjacent; Sheweth, that your poor Petitioners, though of the weaker sex, do too sensibly perceive the ensuing desolation of this kingdom, unless by some timely means Your Honours provide for the speedy recovery thereof. Your Honours are the physicians, that can, by God's special blessing (which we humbly implore), restore this languishing nation, and our bleeding sister, the kingdom of Ireland, which hath now breathed almost her last gasp. We need not dictate to your eagle-eyed judgments the way; our only desire is that God's glory in the true Reformed Protestant Religion may be preserved; the just prerogatives and privileges of King and Parliament maintained; the true liberties and properties of the subject, according to the known laws of the land, restored; and all honourable ways and means for a speedy peace endeavoured. May it, therefore, please Your Honours that some speedy course may be taken for the settlement of the true Reformed Protestant religion for the glory of God, and the renovation of trade for the benefit of the subject, they being the soul and body of the kingdom. And your Petitioners, with many millions of afflicted souls, groaning under the burden of these times of distress, shall (as bound) pray, etc." (Cobbett's "Parliamentary History of England." L., 1808, Vol. III., p. 160).

carried on to a large extent by petitions to Parliament. Women took part in them from the first. So they figure in the petitions got up in the country on account of Catholic Emancipation.[1]

(2) In France, since 1789, and especially during the Revolution, women were not lax in using the right of petition. At one particular time there was an attempt made to take it away from them, namely, in 1851. The friends of the Prince-President, the future Emperor Napoleon III., started, by means of petitions, an agitation for the revision of the Constitution, with the object of repealing the rule which made the President incapable of re-election. To checkmate this agitation, a Bill on the exercise of the right of petition was submitted to the National Assembly, with a view to prevent factious expression of opinion. Article 9 of the Bill

[1] At the sitting of 19th February, 1829, in the House of Lords, Lord Eldon, in presenting several petitions against any further concessions to the Catholics, said that there was one petition that he did not well know how to treat, for it was signed by several ladies; that he was not aware that there was any precedent to exclude the ladies from their Lordship's House, but that he would look into the journals and see whether there existed any precedent to prevent the ladies from forwarding their remonstrances to that House against measures which they considered injurious to the Constitution. Lord King inquired whether the petition expressed the sentiments of young or old ladies. Lord Eldon said he could not answer the noble lord as to that point, but of this he was sure, that there were many women who possessed more knowledge of the Constitution and more common sense than the descendants of chancellors. (Lord King was descended from Lord Chancellor King.) To which Lord King replied he was sure the sentiments expressed in the petition were those of the old women in England. (Hansard, 1829, vol. xx., p. 372., etc.)

provided "that women and minors cannot address petitions to the National Assembly, except for redress of personal grievances." This Bill was vigorously opposed by several members of the Left. Laurent (of the Ardéche) opened the attack. "The Constitution of 1848," said he, "made the right of petition a universal right—the only universal right. It ought to make it especially the right of those to whom it granted no other rights. . . . For electors, the right of petition is only an accessory or supplementary power, whilst it is the principal, the one and only resource of citizens, who are deprived of political rights, and who cannot find in voting at elections a natural, a peaceable opportunity for saying what they think, or what they feel, or what they fear. . . Well! it is these persons that the political law excludes from sovereignty and reduces to the simple position of petitioners, that you now wish to deprive of the right of petition. The Constitution has left them this only, and you wish to take it away. The question is not as to the exercise of political sovereignty, but as to the exercise of a natural right. . . Keep scrupulously, if you will, the monopoly of official sovereignty, but do not make too much of the autocrats, and, at least, allow those who live under our laws to tell us what they think of our Government."

The reporter of the Bill replied that it was a matter of public decency and parliamentary dignity. "What would happen? A petition would arrive, signed in one sense by the husband, and in another sense by the wife. Which authority and which sex would prevail here? . . . If the right of political petition was given to women, it was not the most distinguished or the best educated women who would petition, be sure of that." [1]

At the second reading of the Bill,[2] M. Schœlcher proposed an amendment to limit the right of petition of minors only, and to maintain that of women in its integrity. Noticing the language of the reporter, he began by remarking that decency had nothing to do with the matter. "The question was not about giving women political rights; but, apart from politics, are there not a thousand questions on which women can have valuable information and on which it would be very wise to consult them, especially on matters which they were permitted to occupy themselves with, as, for example, primary education, poor relief. Women," said he, in conclusion, "could therefore keep the right of petition without being involved in the heat of politics, and they ought to retain it in consideration of the very part that society had assigned to them outside politics." Crémieux (who was one of the founders of the Second Republic, and its first Minister of Justice), was not less energetic in supporting the right of women to retain the power of political petition. Finally, the Assembly decided in favour of M. Schœlcher's amendment. But in the end the whole Bill came to nothing.

§ 3.—Right of Meeting and of Association.

(1) The right of free meeting and of association, proclaimed in France by the Revolution, and blended with one another from the first by law and practice

[1] Sitting of 23rd June ("Moniteur" of 24th June, 1851).

[2] Sitting of 2nd July ("Moniteur" of 3rd July, 1851).

alike, is the right which women have most used and abused. The participation of women in Jacobin clubs and other revolutionary societies, as well as their own clubs, and their open air gatherings, were some of the most powerful factors of material and moral disorder which characterised that epoch. I have already had occasion to mention how the Terrorists, weary of their female allies, enjoined them to go back to their homes, and not to meddle any further with public affairs. And in order that this intimation should not prove ineffectual, the Convention challenged the exercise by women of the right of meeting and association. In the speech already cited, in which Amar denounced political women before the Convention, he delivered himself of a curious doctrinal examination of the right of political association and the right of women to take part in it. "The object of popular associations is to unmask the manœuvres of the enemies of the Republic, and to keep an eye on citizens as individuals and on public officers, as well as on the legislative body; to stimulate the zeal of both by the example of republican virtues, and to enlighten them by searching public discussions on the defect or the reformation of political laws. Can women devote themselves to these useful and laborious duties?" To this question the speaker replies in the negative, first because of the difference between the sexes in strength and physical constitution, and consequently in their respective destination. "And, then, does the modesty of women allow them to appear in public, to argue with men, and to discuss before the people questions on which the safety of the Republic depends? . . Besides, when we consider that the political education of men is still in its dawning, that the principles are not yet fully developed, and that we still lisp the word liberty, there is still more reason to say that women, whose moral education is almost a blank, are still worse informed in the first principles. We may add that women, from their organisation, are disposed to an exaltation which would be dangerous in public affairs, and that the interests of the State would soon be sacrificed to all the aberration and disorder that the vivacity of their passions is likely to produce. Thrown into the heat of public debate, they would inculcate in their children's minds not a patriotic spirit, but spite and prejudice." The Convention was won over to the arguments adduced, and decided on the suppression of women's clubs. In vain did Charlier maintain with considerable force that women were free to assemble, and that "unless it could be proved, as in an ancient council of the Church, that women do not form part of mankind, you could not take away this right, which is common to every thinking person." This argument of natural right was met with a still more peremptory argument, *viz.*, that of revolutionary right. "You have thrown," said Bazire, "for a moment a veil over principles, for fear of the abuse that might be made of them to bring upon us a counter-revolution. The only question, therefore, is whether associations of women are dangerous. Experience has shown in the recent past how injurious they are to public peace. This being granted, do not speak of principles. I demand, as a revolutionary measure and as a measure of public safety, that, at all events during the Revolution, these associations be forbidden." The Convention decreed forthwith (9th Brumaire in the 2nd year of the Republic), that female clubs and associations, whatever their designation might be, should be suppressed.

Some months later, after having been deprived of the right of association, women had also the right of meeting taken away from them. On the 4th Prairial of the 3rd year (23rd May, 1794), the Convention decreed that women could not attend at any political meeting. Another decree of the same day commanded women to retire to their homes, and ordered the arrest of those who were found gathered in groups of more than five persons. In addition, the admission of women to the galleries of the House of the National Convention was forbidden until calm should be restored in Paris (decree of 1st Prairial in the 3rd year).

(2) When the right of meeting and of association was restored in their honour after the Revolution of February, women hastened to take advantage of it. On this occasion also they only succeeded in carrying to the highest pitch the excesses in the use of the right of meeting which were committed in 1848.[1] The proclamation

[1] The people rose in defence of the right of meeting ; and the day after the victory every one wished to meet ; everywhere clubs were opened. There was no system, political or social, left unnoticed. Every one present spoke on every subject, ventilating his ideas, and wishing to force them upon other people. There was frantic cheering and hissing. There was crowding and pushing, and general excitement with bustle and noise. Every one wanted to see and hear and talk. Every one expounded his dreams and put forward his plans. Never were imaginations a prey to such confusion. It was like a fever which burst in epidemic form on the whole population and struck it with delirium. There being not enough clubs for them under a roof, they got up numerous clubs in the open air. In the market places, at the corners of streets, at day and at night, poor and rich, workmen and bourgeois,

of the Provisional Government of the 15th April, declared clubs "a necessity for the republic and a citizen's right." When, soon after, the National Assembly thought fit, whilst regulating the right, to restrain the necessity, it found that for women the necessity did not exist at all. Accordingly Article 3 of the decree of 28th July (2nd August), 1848, provided that women could not be members of a club nor attend at it. The discussion in the Chamber on this article was very short. A member remarked that as the law, by regulating the holding of public meetings, takes every reasonable precaution in the interests of public order and morals, there was no reason to prevent women from attending at these meetings; otherwise, he went on to say that it would be necessary also to exclude them from the right of assisting at the sittings of the National Assembly. But these observations did not meet with any support.[1]

(3) As to the present French law on the right of association, women, like men, are under the drag of Articles 291 and 294 of the Penal Code, which forbid the formation of all associations, political or non-political, of more than twenty persons without the sanction of Government. The right of meeting is regulated by the

women and children loitered, gathered in crowds, argued, speechified, and became intoxicated with talk and passions. (Garnier Pagès, "Histoire de la Revolution de 1848," t. vi., p. 174).

[1] The measure which shut the door of the clubs against women received a hearty welcome from public opinion, because, as a well-known novelist wrote, "In the clubs they would have at length lost the few remaining graces which distinguish them from men. For some time it is not perhaps a bad thing that there should be two sexes; later on we may reconsider this point." (Quoted by Faure and Fontaine, in "Le peuple et la place publique," P., 1869, p. 159.)

law of 20th June, 1881, which, whilst it leaves public meetings free, requires a preliminary declaration by two persons enjoying civil and *political* rights, as to the place, day and hour of meeting (Art. 2). Then women cannot make this declaration. The right of attending at public meetings is not denied them by the law. But if the meeting is convened as an "electoral meeting," with the object of selecting candidates for public offices, and receiving their addresses, women may not attend, for only electors of the division, members of the two Houses, and agents of the candidates can take part in electoral meetings (Art. 5).

(4) As to other countries of the Continent, the right of association and of meeting is limited with regard to women in Germany and Austria. Article 4 of the Constitution of the German Empire has reserved the regulation of the right of association for Imperial legislation, but, as hitherto no federal law on the subject has been enacted, the particular provisions of the several countries of the Empire remain still in force. The Prussian law of 11th March, 1850, forbids women being admitted as members of associations, "which have for their object to discuss at their meetings political matters." They are likewise forbidden to attend at the sittings and meetings of these associations (Sec. 8) under pain of a fine of 5 to 50 thalers (Sec. 16). Similar provisions are also found in the Bavarian law of 26th February, 1850 (Sec. 15), in the law of Saxony of 22nd November, 1850 (Sec. 22), and in that of Brunswick of 4th July, 1853. In Austria, too, the law on the right of meeting, of 15th November, 1867, provides that women cannot be members of political associations (Sec. 30).

§ 4.—Liberty of the Press.

(1) The principle of the liberty of the press, although recognised nearly everywhere now, is subject to certain restrictions in some countries, as regards the periodical political press. The State has given up the guarantees which it used to require in the shape of previous authorisation, security, or stamp duty. But in order to be able to reach periodical publications, in case they should transgress the common law, the legislations of several countries require the appointment for each publication of a special representative, who, should it become necessary, can be held responsible, and who ought properly to be the man who edits the publication and on whom consequently depends the printing or non-printing of objectionable articles. This person, called manager, or editor, or responsible publisher, must combine certain qualifications. Is sex one of them?

(2) In France the Press Law of 1828 required a responsible manager, who must have the qualification stipulated by Article 980 of the Civil Code, that is to say, he must be of the male sex. These provisions of 1828 were considered to be still in force under the law of 11th May, 1868. The law of the 29th July, 1881, which at present regulates the press, enacts that "the manager must be a Frenchman of full age, having the enjoyment of his civil rights, and must not be deprived of his civic rights by any sentence of a court" (Art. 6). As there is no reservation in the text of the law in respect of the sex of the manager, we are allowed to draw the conclusion that women have the legal capacity of assuming

these duties. The Keeper of the Seals was, therefore, fully justified in declaring, in his circular of 9th November, 1881, that, the conditions of former legislation on the subject of the sex of the manager having been omitted, "women could now fill the post of manager."[1] But married women, not having the power of entering into engagements, could not assume the duties of manager unless authorised by their husbands.

(3) The latest Press Laws in Germany and Austria have placed women in the same position. The law of the German Empire, of the 7th May, 1874, only requires that the "responsible editor" should be an independent person in possession of civil rights and residing within the Empire (Sec. 8). German commentators (Fr. v. Liszt,[2] Berner,[3] P. Kayser,[4] and Marquardsen[5]), agree on the point that women are not excluded by this law.

[1] Comp. "Code expliqué de la presse," by G. Barbier, (P., 1887), t. 1., p. 90, who, whilst not condemning this interpretation, finds that the formula of the law is not at all clear, and that the preparatory legislative labours are far from throwing any light on this rather obscure point; for the reporter of the law to the Senate stated that Article 6 did not exclude woman from the post of manager; whilst the reporter to the Chamber of Deputies remarked that the law required of the manager only "certain conditions of nationality, age, *sex*, and civil capacity." According to the doctrine which I have set up with regard to the enjoyment of individual public rights, as distinguished from political rights, I am of opinion that the very silence of the law is a peremptory reason in favour of women.

[2] "Das deutsche Reichspressrecht" (Berlin, 1880), p. 38.

[3] "Lehrbuch des deutschen Pressrechts" (Leipzig, 1876), p. 214.

[4] "Das Pressrecht." Appendix to the Handbook of German Penal Law edited by Holtzendorf (Berlin, 1877), p. 583.

[5] "Das Reichs-Press-Gesetz" of 7th May, 1874, with Introduction and Commentaries (Berlin, 1875), p. 78.

Marquardsen, who was the reporter of the law to the Reichstag, says that "in the new Imperial Press Law equality of women with the male sex in that respect is tacitly recognised."

The Austrian Law, of 17th December, 1862 (Sec. 12) requires that the "responsible editor" must be *sui juris* (*eigenberechtigt*), whence the same conclusion is drawn that women are capable of holding this office.[1]

On the other hand, we find in the Spanish and Bulgarian Laws express provisions which exclude women from the responsible management of periodicals. The Spanish Law of 26th July, 1883, requires that the publisher of periodicals, in making his declaration, should sign that he is in full possession of his civil *and political* rights. Now, these latter do not belong to women.

In the same way the Bulgarian Law of 17-29th December, 1887, stipulates that every Bulgarian subject enjoying civil *and political* rights "may become publisher or editor."

Lastly, in Russia and Finland, only persons approved by Government can be publishers and responsible editors. The Censorship Laws, which regulate the press there (Russian Law of 6th April, 1865, Finland Ordinance of 31st May, 1867), make no reservation as to the sex of these persons, but in both countries there are several precedents in favour of women.

[1] Fr. v. Liszt, "Lehrbuch des Œsterreichischen Pressrechts," (Leipzig, 1878), p. 135.

§ 5.—Liberty of Instruction.

(1) Between the two categories of individual rights which I have pointed out, those of a public character (right of petition, association, and meeting, and liberty of the press), and those of a private character (individual liberty, liberty of conscience, inviolability of the home), may be placed certain liberties which partake of the one and the other set. The exercise of these liberties carries the citizen outside his private existence; but in the external sphere, to which he is transported, his activity preserves a private character; it has no direct influence, or perhaps no influence at all on the State. These liberties are the liberty of instruction and the liberty of professions.

The liberty of instruction, which is sanctioned by nearly all modern constitutions, but is in practice observed with less unanimity, is not affected by difference of sex. If the State thinks that it ought to assume the monopoly of instruction, it establishes it against all, and *vice versâ* when it gives it up, it does not exclude women more than men. Side by side with the liberty of instruction, which consists in the unrestricted power of teaching, there is also put forward the liberty of not following public instruction, the right of the student to choose his own course of studies at the university, the right of a *paterfamilias* to choose a school for his children—a denominational or an undenominational, a public or a private school. But while putting forward the "liberty of not following public instruction," one generally forgets the liberty of following public instruction, the liberty of learning, perhaps because one thinks that it is comprised in the natural right of equality before the law. It would, however, deserve a place of its own, if it were only on account of the restrictions which it has undergone in the past. At Rome, Julian the Apostate forbade the higher studies to his "Galilean" subjects. In the Middle Ages bastards could not aspire to the degree of Doctor of Divinity. Until quite a recent period the Universities of Oxford and Cambridge were closed to persons who did not belong to the Established Church. In Russia, even in the present day, Polish Catholics, and especially Jews, are not admitted to certain schools, or only in limited numbers fixed beforehand.

(2) What is the position of women from the point of view of liberty of instruction? On principle we must recognise that in cases where public schools are kept up at the cost of the nation, all its members have a right to use them in the same way as they use the courts of law, the post and telegraph, and other public institutions. But as instruction in schools is received in common and not separately, there may arise inconveniences and dangers to decency and public morality, from intercourse between the sexes, before they arrive at years of discretion, so it may be required that the liberty of following public instruction should be limited as regards females, more especially in schools of intermediate education. But with regard to higher education which is followed by grown up persons in full possession of their responsibility, the reasons given for restricting the liberty of women's public education are insufficient. In times not very remote from our own, when woman was considered sufficiently learned, to use the words of the classical

character of Molière's play,[1] if she could distinguish a doublet from a trunk hose, the question of admitting women to the universities was idle. So that the laws and regulations on higher education were, so to speak, taken unawares, when the movement for the emancipation of women was set on foot. In the absence of express provisions, what ought to be the solution of the problem? The doctrine which we have invariably followed in respect of the enjoyment of individual, as distinct from political rights, as well as the special considerations just advanced, forbid our answering the question of the admissibility of women to the universities and high schools otherwise than in the affirmative. But in admitting them to the lectures and examinations for degrees, the State, of course, does not pledge itself to open for them public careers under the same conditions as it does to men. If women claimed as much, the same doctrine which brought us to recognise their right of instruction with all its effects in the domain of education would tell against them. The State owes them education to develop their intellectual culture, according to their inclinations and the congeniality of their minds, but if they ask for education to enable them to fill an office or practise a profession, they do it at their own risk.

(3) It is in this way, which appears to me the only just

[1] Il n'est pas bien honnête, et pour beaucoup de causes,
Q'une femme étudie et sache tant de choses.

. . . .

Nos pères, sur ce point, étaient gens bien sensés,
Qui disaient qu'une femme en sait toujours asses
Quand la capacité de son esprit se hausse
A connaitre un pourpoint d'avec un haut-de-chausse.
(*Les femmes savantes*, Acte II., Scene VII).

and correct one, that the French Universities took up the question when it was raised. France was, perhaps, the only country which adopted this solution of the problem from the outset. Already under the Second Empire women were admitted not only to follow the courses of lectures but to obtain university degrees. The other countries are still far from having adopted this line. In some, Ordinances or Royal decrees have opened the universities to women. It was so in Sweden by the decree of 3rd June, 1870. The other portion of the Scandinavian monarchy, Norway, by the law of 14th June, 1884, adopted a still broader measure, by assimilating female students to male students, not only as regards their right to enter for university examinations and to take academical degrees, but also as regards their enjoyment of scholarships and endowments bequeathed to the university.[1] In Denmark, an ordinance of 25th June, 1875, gave to women the *right of academic citizenship*, with the power to obtain degrees except in the Faculty of Theology, but without the right to receive subsidy or assistance from the university.[2] In Italy, women have been admitted to all the universities of the kingdom, by virtue of a university regulation of 8th October, 1876. The Swiss universities, one after another, and even the ultra-conservative University of Bâsle, opened their doors to women. The new Belgian Law of 10th April, 1890, on the subject of conferring degrees, has expressly decided that women can obtain academical degrees (Art 52). In England, the University of London and the Victoria University are the only ones to confer degrees

[1] "Annuaire de législ, compar.," xiv., 611.
[2] "Annuaire," v., 801.

on women. The old Universities of Oxford and Cambridge still hold them at arm's length; but under their shade have sprung up special colleges for women, Girton College in 1872, and Newnham College, in 1875, at Cambridge, and Lady Margaret Hall and Somerville Hall at Oxford (opened in 1879). The students of these colleges are admitted to the university examinations, but are not granted the degrees. In addition to those colleges, there is also in London a special school of medicine for women. An ordinance issued in 1892 by the Scottish University Commissioners has empowered these universities to admit women to instruction and graduation. As yet the operation of the ordinance has been confined to the Faculty of Arts. In the University of Edinburgh women and men are admitted to the same class-rooms, while in the University of Glasgow the women are taught separately from the men. The University of St. Andrews has instituted, as early as in 1877, special degrees in Arts for women. For Ireland, the New University Act (1879) granted to the Dublin University power to confer upon women degrees in secular subjects. High schools exclusively for women have been founded in Italy (Rome and Florence), and Russia. In the latter country there was a school of medicine, which has been suppressed (some years ago, but it is likely to be reopened), and there are still two or three high schools for general culture of ladies. In Germany and Austria the universities are, generally speaking, closed to women.[1] In the English colonies women are everywhere admitted to the benefits of higher education. In the United States

[1] It appears that some of these universities, too, are prepared to admit to their class-rooms women, especially so in South Germany.

the practice varies; the universities, sprung from private foundations, do not always admit women. This is the case, for example, at Johns Hopkins' University,[1] but the State universities are more liberal; the right of women to be admitted to them is sometimes even provided for by the Constitution.[2]

§ 6.—Liberty of Professions.

Professions, the exercise of which is not regulated by law, are for that very reason outside our inquiry. As to the professions in respect of which the legislator thinks fit to impose a test of ability, the claim of women to exercise them ought to be decided according to whether they possess the established proof of capacity or not. If the standard required is the diploma of a specified school, women who have obtained the diploma, ought clearly to be allowed to practise the profession. With regard to *public offices*, the diploma is only one of the conditions required to fill them, and, besides, it is only an accessory condition, which comes after certain others, as, for example, the enjoyment of political rights, whilst for the State-regulated professions it is *the* condition. As soon as the guarantee of the diploma, which is required in the interests of society, is fulfilled, all the other qualities or properties of the person who possesses it are of no interest to the State; it is the individual's business to make his choice between the persons who hold the diploma. Then (save for exceptions, which

[1] It has recently authorised a woman to follow the courses of lectures without the right to compete for a degree (*Nation*, review published at New York, of 1st October, 1891).

[2] Compare the Constitution of California, art. ix., sec. 9.

should not be admitted but on a plea), is not sex one of the contingent qualities as regards the exercise of trades and professions? If it is not so according to the manners of the day, the question, every time it arises in practice, will be silently decided in compliance with those manners, so that the intervention of the public authority is in this case superfluous. If, on the contrary, the prevailing opinion is against any restriction of the liberty of professions by reason of sex, by what right is the State to step in to establish such distinctions? We must, therefore, admit that the right of women to practise equally with men professions, not invested with a public character, ought to be recognised as not requiring any express authorisation from the law.

However, in some countries such permissive provisions have been made allowing women to practise as physicians, druggists, etc. That occurred in England, Holland, Belgium, Sweden, and Russia,[1] generally by means of ordinances or decrees.

[1] The English Law of 1876, allowing the registration of women under the Medical Act (39 and 40 Vict., c. 41); the Belgian Law of 10th April, 1890 (art. 24, 25, 52), recognising the right of women to practise as physicians and apothecaries; the Imperial Russian Ordinance of 2nd August, 1890, relating to female physicians; the Decree of November, 1870, in the Netherlands, to the effect of admitting women to practise as apothecaries, etc.

In some countries where women, not being allowed to take university degrees and diplomas, are debarred from professions, the exercise of which depends on those diplomas, personal exceptions have been made by the gracious act of the sovereign. Thus the Emperor of Austria authorised a woman to practise as a physician, in virtue of the diploma obtained by her at a foreign university (*Cf.* Gumplowicz, "Das œsterreichische Staatsrecht," Vienna, 1891, p. 97).

For the most part, these measures were enacted, one may say, in deference to traditions, which did not admit that women could devote themselves to professions which were considered as masculine, because hitherto men only had practised them. The effect of these decrees and ordinances in point was to establish formally the fact of the advent of new notions and new conditions of social life carrying with them new social arrangements.

CHAPTER VI.

Quasi-Public Rights attached to Civil Capacity.

(1) THE question of the liberty of professions, which concluded our examination of public individual rights, has brought us to the extreme limit of those external appearances of man in society which belong to public law. If we pass this line, we shall at once find ourselves in the sphere of man's private activity, which forms the domain of civil law. Nevertheless, there have been arrayed on the frontier line, certain rights which, though *civil* in their origin and nature, have been declared *public,* in order that they might be reserved for those only who have the enjoyment of public rights. This classification dates from antiquity.

" The ancient legislations chose to associate with public rights a certain number of purely civil rights, in order to forbid them to women, and they called them *officia virilia.* The several rights so styled were those, the practice of which would have carried woman along, if not in public life, at all events in outside life, and would bring her out of the *gynecaeum* or the *atrium,* where ancient customs kept her confined. Although French notions in this respect have never borne a resemblance to those of the ancients, our old jurists, who would willingly have remodelled the whole of society on the Roman model, remained closely wedded to the doctrine of the Pandects, and inscribed on our customs the old adage, 'Woman should guard the house, the fire, and the children.'"[1]

The modern legislator proved himself unable to extricate himself from these ideas. He hallowed these prejudices by excluding women from the duties of witness to a deed and of a guardian.

What is really the nature of these duties? The witness to a deed is one who attests and confirms by his signature a fact within his knowledge, that it may be recorded in a public document, that is to say, in an act of pure civil law, drawn up with the concurrence of a public officer. If the witnesses contribute to the solemnity of the proceedings before the public officer, they certainly do not confer the solemn form on the deed; it is the public officer who invests it with this, on the faith of the facts attested by the witnesses. It is, therefore, incorrect to say that "the witnesses represent society."[2] It is not at all the mission of society to follow all the concrete facts concerning individuals. Still more erroneous is the opinion, in accordance with which "the witnesses find themselves for the moment to be the depositaries of public authority."[3] It is the public officer alone who is the depositary of public authority, by virtue of the power delegated to him by the chief of the State or his Minister, and who, in this capacity, gives the stamp of authenticity to the deed which he receives, and imparts to it a form which gives it an executory

[1] P. Gide, "Etude sur la condition privée de la femme" (Paris, 2nd edition, 1885), p. 421.

[2] F. Laurent, "Principes de Droit Civil" (1870), ii., p. 40.

[3] "Massé et Vergé sur le Droit Civil Français de Zachariae" (P. 1857), t. iii., p. 102.

force. The witnesses are only the depositaries of the material facts which they supply to the public officer.

Guardianship is a substitution for paternal authority which the minor happens to be in want of. Its object is the education of the child and the administration of his property, both being duties of a strictly private character. It is only the conditions under which the guardian enters on his duties that impart to them a public character. He is appointed, not by private agreement, but by virtue of the law, and he has no right to decline the duty, which is thus a *munus publicum,* and places him under the supervision and the more or less extended control of the public authorities. The Roman law considered that guardianship itself was *vis ac potestas publica.* Modern law has not taken the trouble to understand the difference between duties exercised under the eye of the State and State functions, and it has sanctioned the old tradition which passed over the woman as guardian, because she was excluded from public power. The Code Napoleon so decided in Article 442, not only as to the duty of guardian, but also as to that of member of a "family council" (which assists and directs the guardian).

(2) By the French Civil Code, in the first place, women are incapable of being witnesses to the certificates of births, deaths, and marriages (Art. 37), and in this respect the Code derogates from the law of 20th September, 1792, which provided that witnesses might be "of either sex." Being allowed to make a "statement" of the fact of birth before the Registrar, women are unable to affix their signatures to "testify" the birth. The reason

of this singular piece of juridical ingenuity was given, during the discussion of the second draft of the Civil Code, by Thibaudeau in the following terms:—"Witnesses are called, not to attest the fact of the birth, but to give to the Act a solemn form."[1] How indefensible this construction is in juridical logic I have already shown by proving that witnesses contribute only to the solemnity of the procedure, but do not confer a solemn form on the Act. If, instead of two witnesses required by law, there were two thousand witnesses, would this assembly, which would certainly not be wanting in solemnity, be sufficient to "give a solemn form to the instrument" without the intervention of a public officer?

(3) In the countries which accepted the Code Napoleon, a reaction set in some time ago against the exclusion of women from being witnesses to deeds. So, in Italy, the law of 9th December, 1877, annulled at one bout all the clauses incapacitating women from being witnesses. It declares that "all the provisions of the law which forbid women to attest as witnesses to public and private deeds are hereby repealed." The Minister of Justice, who at that time was the celebrated lawyer, Mancini, in defending the Bill before the Chamber, said:—"The right of attesting is a natural right. Why, then, deprive the woman of it? Since you give her the name of citizen, can you refuse her one of the least of the privileges of a citizen? We are at Rome; it would be sad if the civilised world should come to

[1] See on the history of Article 37 an interesting paper by M. Paul Viollet, "Les temoins mâles" (Nouvelle Revue Historique de droit français et étranger, 1890, No. 5, p. 715).

think that we are following in the track of the old Roman laws."[1]

The Island of Mauritius has made the same reform in its Civil Code, which she has received from France.

In Canada, in the French speaking province of Quebec, women are admitted to witness wills by private deed, under the condition that there should be at least two witnesses present, both at the same time, and attesting in the presence and at the request of the testator (Art. 851 of the Civil Code).

The most recent Civil Code, that of Spain (of 24th July, 1889), maintained the exclusion of women from guardianship (Art. 237), and from being witnesses (Art. 681), but it made, however, an exception in regard to the latter in case of epidemic, when "a will can be made, without the concurrence of a notary, before three witnesses, above sixteen years of age, men or women" (Art. 701).

We find similar provisions in Austria as regards guardians[1] and witnesses;[2] while the admission of women to witness "privileged wills" is somewhat wider. By virtue of Article 597 of the Civil Code, "women of fourteen years, at least, can witness wills made at sea or in places where the plague or other contagious diseases are raging."

Germany is on the eve of obtaining a new Civil Code

[1] Sitting of March 26, 1877.

[2] Secs. 192, 198 of the Civil Code. (Das allgemeine Bürgerliche Gesetzbuch.)

[3] *Ibid*, sec. 591. Law relating to notaries, of 25th February, 1871, secs. 55, 57.

for the whole Empire. The old laws on the subject recall the provisions of the Code Napoleon.[1]

The laws of Russia, where women, married or unmarried, enjoy all civil rights, contain no restrictions whatever on the capacity of woman to be guardian or witness to deeds.[2]

[1] Compare, for example, the legislation of Prussia. As to guardians, the Law of 5th July, 1875, secs. 21, 70; as to witnesses, Landrecht der preussischen Staaten, part i., tit. xii., sec. 115; Law about Notaries of 11th July, 1875, sec. 7. Also in Saxony the Law about Notaries of 3rd June, 1859, sec. 18, etc.

[2] Compare Art. 253, 256 of the Civil Laws (Russ. Code, t. x., part i.), and Art. 86 of the Law about Notaries.

CONCLUSION.

(1) We have brought our inquiry to an end. We have examined the laws of the different countries as to the position of woman, in respect of her ability to exercise political and public rights. We have attempted to trace, by the light of history, the successive phases of the movement in favour of *woman's rights* in the different parts of the globe. What conclusions may be drawn from this study in law and history?

Neither the one branch nor the other of our inquiry has provided us with any single solution of the problem involved in woman's claims. No general concession is made to them, nor yet is exception taken to them altogether. The answer varies with the nature of the demands.

The latter, despite their diversity, may be classified under three heads, *viz.* (*a*) political equality, that is, in particular, parliamentary suffrage and eligibility; (*b*) economic emancipation, that is, complete equality for woman before the civil law in the disposal of her person and property, with the free use of all her abilities and means, material and intellectual; (*c*) intellectual emancipation, that is, granting woman the same facilities as man for the cultivation of her intellect, giving her, too, access to all public schools, and to the degrees there conferred, as evidence of the culture acquired.

(2) The verdict of the Law on woman's demand for *political equality* is, we saw reason to think, implied in the very distinction we were led to establish between political rights and individual public rights. Assuming that the latter, which are concerned with the liberty of the individual in all its manifestations, are indispensable to the full development of man in society, we recognised that the free enjoyment of these rights ought to have no other limit than the rightful liberty of other individuals. On the other hand, as to political rights, since participation in the government of the country—which is their very essence—presupposes a special capacity, and is by no means an integral part of human personality, nor requisite to its development, we judged them to be not an absolute, but a relative, right, a creation of law. In fact, "Natural right" is the only obstacle in the way of this conclusion. But, however glorious was the part played by "natural right" as a weapon against despotism, and however great were the services it has thereby rendered to civilisation, it is in reality no more than a theory, which has its foundation in political metaphysics, not in Law; for it is not based on experience, nor does it express any necessary relations of things. The government of the commonweal, not being the personal property of anyone, neither a *caste* privilege, nor yet an hereditary right, is essentially an office performed in the general interest. It can only be conferred, then, by the law interpreting the general interest suitably to the ideas, needs, and even passions and prejudices, of the place and of the time. These factors, which vary with every country and every age, determine the concession of political power, on conditions of more or less liberality,

to a group, wider or narrower in extent, of such inhabitants as are deemed capable, rightly or wrongly, of a proper discharge of the elector's duties. Thus the question of admission to, or exclusion from, the government of a country, is independent of the principles of Law, and confined wholly to the sphere of politics.

It seems to me the more necessary to emphasise this point, as the scientific and popular press, that have done me the honour of noticing my book since its appearance in French, have sometimes characterised my attitude towards female suffrage in the most contradictory terms; while some have regarded me as being opposed to the political emancipation of woman, others have classed me among the partisans of the movement. Despite my lively sense of gratitude towards the eminent savants and publicists of various countries who have reviewed my book with so much friendliness, I cannot but protest against the divergent views attributed to me on this point. As a jurist, I should have exceeded my powers, had I taken part either for or against female suffrage; I should have strained the authority of Law, had I interposed it in a dispute of party politics. My task and duty consisted, in fact, in demonstrating that woman's right to the suffrage, her admission to, or exclusion from, the electorate, far from depending on any general legal principle, was simply a matter of legislation. The general position thus assumed by me has successfully stood the test of the entire legal history of woman's demand for political suffrage, which I have put together. All the facts I have brought into prominence, and in fact the judicial opinion of the old and new worlds, as seen in a series of particular decisions, arrived at for reasons, more or less clearly expressed and felicitously defined, have proved to be in accord with my position. Both partisans and opponents of female suffrage, then, are henceforth called on to quit the domain of Law, and referred, without favour shown to the claim of either side, to the legislator, who, it may be, will arrive at different decisions in different countries, in favour now of one party, now of the other.

(3) Very different is the attitude of the Law towards woman's demand for economic and intellectual emancipation, that is, towards the free development of her personality. As the *raison d'être* and the end of social order is to ensure such free development to every member of the community, whatever his rank, and whatever his moral, intellectual, or material value, it follows that human personality in society is invested, from the outset, with certain rights implied in its very existence and natural need of expansion. So these rights are in no way due to the power of the State. Far from creating them, the law interposes merely to protect or ensure the enjoyment of them. Truly, the rights in question, being the expression of the necessary, actual relations of men in society, cannot, for that very reason, be treated as substantive entities, or as of an absolute nature. The requirements of social life may demand that they should be modified now and again. But such qualifications are only exceptions to the rule; the latter alone is self-evident and incontestable, while the exceptions have to be justified and made the subject of stipulation.

This obvious truth has induced me, in dealing with the problem before us, to propound the following principle of jurisprudence: "When the enjoyment of a public privilege is in dispute, the decision will depend, if individual public rights are concerned, on the existence of a law of restriction; if political rights are concerned, on the existence of a law of concession." This rule, laid down by me as the fundamental principle in the interpretation of public law, has succeeded, as we have seen, in introducing method and order into all the vast confusion of laws and legal controversies about women's rights in different countries, and opened up a clear prospect, as through a forest of thick, interlacing boughs, from end to end of them. It leads directly to the proposition, that every right which is not a public function of *government*, (*i.e.*, not connected with the control of the State or of its organs), is secured beforehand to woman in the same way as to man. Woman, therefore, in respect of her other claims, I mean those not concerned with her political emancipation, need not beg, as a favour, the rights which they imply, but may demand them as her property—hers by as good titles as the other members of the community of whatever sex, race, origin, etc., can produce.

Doubtless, as we have already admitted, society may, in virtue of the powers derived from its very *raison d'être*, create exceptions, or impose limitations on the exercise of any right whatsoever, provided the general interest require it. But the duty of proving such requirement, rests, in the case of individual rights, on society. Whereas, in the case of *political* rights, the individual appears in the rôle of a suitor, he is, with respect to *individual* rights, only a defendant quietly entrenched in his position, which must be conquered to oust him. So situated, he is free of the great burden—the *onus probandi.* That falls with all its weight on society, which may not shift it aside at pleasure, nor yet oppose to it the strength of prejudices, whose only justification is their antiquity. And, is woman, when her exercise of these rights stand in question, to receive a different treatment? Clearly not. Such treatment would be the very negation of Law.

The legal system I have just formulated, if it has logic and theoretical truth on its side, may possibly prove also of some practical utility outside the boundaries of Law. While this system places the discussion on a rational basis, it provides it with the directing hand which may have been lacking in the midst of those manifold considerations—drawn from sentiment, tradition, Christianity, physiology, anatomy, demography, and I know not what else—which were so eagerly accumulated anyhow, by both opponents and supporters of woman's rights, whether her demand for political suffrage, or her aspiration towards intellectual culture, or her admission to some profession or business, was in question. The clue held out by the principles of Law may, perhaps, prove a serviceable one; it brings with it, at least, the assistance of logic, which is never out of place.

So much for the conclusions we derive from Law.

(4) What lessons are taught by the facts brought together in the course of this study?

The legislative movement we have been considering is, doubtless, still distant from its goal; in some respects, indeed, it is only just starting. But, in any case, it is already sufficiently under weigh to enable us to discern the tendencies which guide it. Now, in every part of the globe, where we have attempted to follow its course, one such tendency has always been discernible. The legislator refuses obstinately to grant *political* rights to woman. With one or two insignificant exceptions, woman has nowhere succeeded in obtaining the parliamentary suffrage. She has, indeed, been more fortunate in respect of local self-government; but the municipal vote granted to her in several countries, is by no means a departure from the general attitude of the legislator towards her political rights. My historical inquiry proved that the municipal vote, both by its origin and character, lacks the significance of a political right. Originating in the amorphous state of the mediæval village community, then sanctioned by law, chiefly in recognition of woman's civil capacity and her rank as a holder of property, her vote at local elections is expressive merely of concrete, economic interests, in presence of which the person as such is entirely thrown into the shade. The legislator is so far from regarding the local vote as a first instalment of the political suffrage, that he stops short, in almost every case, at the boundary parting the common interests of a locality from the more important sphere of politics.

While he exhibits such reserve, not to say dislike, towards woman's political claims, the legislator shows himself much more favourably disposed towards her social emancipation, and readier every year to put an end to the state of social inferiority in which she has been kept for centuries by the laws, and, still more, by the influence of popular prejudice. This twofold attitude is nowhere more clearly visible than in the great American democracy of the United States, a society, it is to be remembered, which is free from the traditions and prejudices of the Old World, and renowned for a rather daring spirit that sticks at no obstacle, and is not frightened by paradox. The Americans are removing the social barriers raised against women; they are admitting them, not only to subordinate offices, but to the Bar, nay, even to the Bar of the highest Court in the land, to that of the Supreme Court of the United States.

"No person," say the recent Constitutions, "shall on account of sex be disqualified from entering or pursuing any lawful business, vocation, or profession."

This is the word.

"Popular sentiment is entirely in favour of giving them every chance."[1] But as soon as political suffrage is demanded for women, the American people become refractory. It is in vain that the "natural right" argument is invoked. The atomist theory, according to which each human unit is entitled to its arithmetical quota of political power, is implicitly swept aside by the American people, and formally condemned by its tribunals. "The legal vindication of the natural right of all citizens to vote would, at this stage of popular intelligence, involve the destruction of civil government. . . . The right to vote ought not to be, and is not, an absolute right. The fact that the practical working of this assumed right would be destructive of civilisation is decisive that the right does not exist." Such are the terms of a judgment given in an action on the subject of Woman's Suffrage.

[1] As Mr. Bryce puts it in his remarkable work, "The American Commonwealth," ii., 601.

Old Europe, in its turn, is shaking off the secular dust of its codes. The perpetual tutelage which used to hang over women is suppressed, the free disposition of their property and person secured to them, and their capacity ungrudgingly recognised even beyond the private sphere. In countries with feudal traditions, not only is the woman of noble birth reinstated in her proprietary rights so far as they concern public life, but women of the lower classes become admitted into it on the same grounds. Nearly everywhere in the Germanic and Slavonic world, the woman who has an independent position is allowed to retain it, and to exert it in matters of local self-government, so long as they do not in any way affect the political order. Directly the woman threatens to pass this limit, the barriers which had been removed are almost invariably re-erected.

At the same time the gates of the universities are opening themselves to women; they can share in the work of intellectual culture undertaken by the society of which they form an integral part. Greater and greater facility is given to them to utilise, for practical ends, the knowledge thus acquired if they lie under a necessity to do so. The State employs them in its service, and confers on them or acknowledges them to have the right of applying themselves to the liberal professions which have hitherto been closed to them. Thus more or less complete satisfaction has been given to woman's demand as expressed by the Frenchwomen of 1789: "We want to be enlightened, and to have employments open to us not in order to usurp the authority of men, but that we may be more highly esteemed by them, and that, if misfortune overtake us, we may have the means of livelihood." In some countries more than in others hesitation or slowness to advance in this direction is shown; but, generally speaking, the movement is already well advanced, and the general conclusion to be drawn from the facts is that the majority of civilised societies are engaged in securing the intellectual and economic emancipation of woman, while setting aside her political equality with men.

The demand for this equality began in the Anglo-Saxon world at a time when the woman possessed neither intellectual freedom nor economic equality in the eyes of the civil law. The married woman especially was weighed down by all the prejudice of the old common law, which refused her any separate existence and adopted the rule that "the wife was merged in her husband." The technical phraseology of the English common law, equally with that of French customary law, employed the designation of *baron* and *femme* for members of the matrimonial community. The former exercised over the latter the rights of lord; she was nothing but his humble vassal. In the United States prior to 1848, in England up to a still more recent date, the husband was master of his wife's real estate and chattels, usufructuary of all her economic interests during coverture, and even after his wife's death he retained for his life the use of her personalty, if there were children, issue of the marriage. In the United States, so recently as in 1860, the father could by will take the custody of his infant children from the surviving mother and give them to whom he pleased.

In the end woman has revolted; she has demanded not only redress of her grievances but, further, by way of reparation and still more of guarantee, a share of political power.

For more than twenty years the legislator has been occupied in England and the United States in reforming the old civil laws with regard to women, and in redressing their grievances. And if, generally speaking, the social emancipation of woman is not yet completed in these countries, there is not very much left to be done there in respect of her civil position—though of several other civilised countries the same could hardly be said.[1]

(5) Whether in the future the legislator persists or not in his present attitude with regard to the political emancipation of women, of which he is the sole and supreme judge, he at all events has a still graver responsibility and duty towards the yet unsettled claims of woman relative to her development in the social sphere that lies beyond the domain of public order. As the fundamental principles of Law do not allow the legislator to interfere in that particular sphere save in exceptional and urgent cases, he is under an obligation to sweep away the obstacles which he placed in the way of woman's activity, if he can no longer justify them on the ground of the general interest of the community in the existing state of civilisation. Where such restrictions are no longer justifiable, any delay on the part of the legislator in suppressing them only tends to injure the general interest which he pretends to serve, and gratuitously to offend those who have to endure them.

[1] On the civil condition of women in continental countries, see Appendix II.

THE END.

APPENDICES

APPENDIX I.

The St. Simonians and Woman's Rôle.

As is commonly known, the St. Simonians were the adherents of a school of social reform founded by the Count de St. Simon for the reconstruction of society, in a religious spirit, for the benefit of the suffering masses. One of their dogmas was equality of woman. They were brought round to it by the double path of sensualism, with which they invested moral order, and their peculiar conception of social order. Christianity, which used to exercise spiritual sway in the world, has lost its power, said the St. Simonians; it has committed the fatal error of confining itself to the spiritual side of things and in looking with disfavour on the material side of life. To direct society, religion ought to embrace the whole social life, and to combine the two elements of which it is composed—the spiritual and the material. The pleasures of the senses, the beauty of the person, ought to be regarded as instruments of moral influence and no longer as sources of evil and sin. This "rehabilitation of the flesh," proclaimed by the St. Simonians, cancelled the condemnation passed by Christian asceticism on woman, who had been regarded as an inferior being, and as the source and cause of the lower passions.

The rank of woman was besides considerably raised by the assumption that in the social order, according to the St. Simonian idea, the woman was inseparable from the man, so that the primordial element of society was not man alone nor woman alone, but man and woman together. In the social hierarchy, composed of successive groups governed by established authorities, all public offices ought therefore to be held by a man and a woman—a pair. So at the head of society there should be a double priest—that is, a priest and priestess. The woman should be everywhere the equal of the man. Marriage must continue to be the foundation of the family, but its ties ought not to be so indissoluble as they are in the Christian society. The question as to how far marriage ties might be relaxed at will became the subject of the greatest divergencies of opinion in the St. Simonian school. Enfantin, who shared with Bazard the guidance of the school, propounded an audacious theory on the relations of the sexes. This theory laid down that there were two kinds of temperaments—the one with deep lasting affections, the other with lively, changeable, and transient affections. To give satisfaction to every nature, marriage ought not to have in the new society the same rigid form that it was now invested with. There ought to be on the one hand a permanent marriage for those whose affections were lasting, and a temporary marriage for those whose affections were transient. Both unions would be sanctioned and dissolved by the double priesthood, which would intervene in the relations between the sexes to regulate the carnal appetites, and for this purpose would not only make use of its moral authority but also of the power of beauty on the senses. Sometimes the priesthood (man and woman) would calm the inconsiderate ardour of the intellect or moderate irregular sensual desires; sometimes it would wake up the apathetic intellect or rekindle torpid desires. This doctrine was repudiated by one party in the school, and was not put into practice by those who remained faithful to Enfantin. But even before the doctrine was formulated, public rumour had imputed to the St. Simonians promiscuous intercourse of the sexes, or possession of women in common. The school explained its ideas relating to women in an address presented to the Chamber of Deputies in 1830.

"Christianity," said the St. Simonians in this document, "has rescued women from slavery, but it has condemned them, nevertheless, to a subordinate position, and everywhere in Christian Europe we see them laid under a religious, political, and civil interdict. The object of the St. Simonians is to announce their positive deliverance, their complete emancipation, but without meaning for that purpose to abolish the sacred law of marriage proclaimed by Christianity; they intend, on the contrary, to fulfil that law, to give it a new sanction, and to add to the force and inviolability of the union which it sanctifies; they require, as the Christians do, that a single man should be united to a single woman, but they teach that the wife should be the equal of the husband, and that in accordance with the particular favour which God has granted to her sex, she should be associated with him in the exercise of the triple function of worship, State, and family, so that the social individual, who up to the present moment has been the man only, should in future be the man *and* the woman. The only object of the religion of St. Simon is to put an end to that disgraceful traffic, that legalises prostitution, which under the name of marriage now frequently sanctions a monstrous union between devotion and egoism, between intelligence and ignorance, between youth and decrepit old age."

Soon after the split which occurred in the sect, Enfantin and forty of his disciples, among whom were some women, retired into his country house at Menilmontant where they put into practice their theories of association in a common life; they one and all gave themselves up to their work, not excepting the hardier and the grosser ones. To remove all false impression of their ideas about marriage and the relations between the sexes, they imposed on themselves the law of celibacy. The Government, however, being of opinion that the St. Simonian sect was dangerous, brought some of its principal members to justice, charging them, among other offences, with an outrage against morality. Before the tribunal one of the accused, Michel Chevalier, the future friend of Richard Cobden, repudiated with the utmost energy the imputation of immorality, and made a counter-accusation against society in whose name the St. Simonians were prosecuted. The principal accused were convicted and sent to prison. The sect continued to exist for a short time. It attempted to reassert itself and to complete its organisation. For if it possessed in the person of Enfantin a high priest, or *Father*, as he was called, they had no priestess or *Mother*, and without her no hierarchy, nor regular government in the *Family* was possible. So the St. Simonians took much trouble to find a *Mother*. The important post was offered to George Sand, the famous novelist, but she refused it. To spread the faith, the *Family* sent to different parts of France and even to foreign countries missionaries, who were also commissioned to find a *Mother*. But they could not find one. Soon the sect dispersed, its members returned to ordinary society, and not a few of them were destined to play an important part in politics, literature and business. The St. Simonians' ideas, especially on economics, have not failed to leave some deep traces on the minds of their generation. But their theories on the emancipation of women and on marriage have not germinated. They have been associated abroad with the doctrine of free love, and have thereby tended to throw into disrepute the cause of female emancipation generally, that is, the removal of women's disabilities both civil and political.

APPENDIX II.

The Civil Condition of Women in France and other Continental Countries.

§ 1.

IN France the civil condition of women varies according to whether they are married or unmarried. Unmarried women are almost entirely relieved from the restrictions which formerly weighed down their sex. Their principal incapacities are those noticed above in the text of this volume, namely the inability of assuming guardianship and that of acting as witnesses to deeds. Their rights over property are the same as the rights of persons of the male sex, that is to say, unmarried women can acquire and freely dispose of their property, can enter into contracts, and sue in law. Before the Revolution, daughters were generally limited in their rights of inheritance, for the benefit of male heirs. Besides, the law, or in its absence, custom, had introduced entails and beforehand renunciation by daughters of their rights of inheritance. The Revolution suppressed the inheritance privilege of the male sex, and subsequent laws have forbidden entails and renunciation of future successions, so that equal rights are secured in a family to daughters as to sons.

The case of the married woman is altogether different. Directly she marries she falls under the absolute power of her husband. The provisions of the Code which created this position for the woman were drawn up under the direct influence of Napoleon. As is well known, his views on the position of woman in society were those of an Oriental despot, for whom woman exists only as an ornament of his seraglio. In his capacity of a man of war, he added to the duties of woman that of furnishing soldiers to the army. A husband, said Napoleon, ought to have an absolute control over the actions of his wife. He has a right to say to her, "Madam, you shall not go out," "Madam, you shall not go to the theatre," "Madam, you shall not see this or that person," in other words, "Madam, you belong to me body and soul." The drawing up of the article providing that the "wife owes obedience to her husband" did not appear to Napoleon sufficiently striking. He asked that the mayor presiding at the marriage ceremony, when pronouncing the legal formularies in presence of the husband and wife, should be clothed in an imposing garb, that he should speak in solemn accents, and that the severe decoration of the hall, imparting the enunciation of that maxim with an awful authority, should impress it for ever on the bride.

The husband's power extends to the person as well as to the property of his wife. The wife is obliged to cohabit with the husband, and to follow him wherever he thinks proper to reside, even if it is at the antipodes. Husband and wife mutually owe fidelity to one another, but infidelity is not estimated by the Penal Code at the same value in the case of the wife as in the case of the husband. The adulterous wife may be imprisoned for a period extending from three months to two years, whilst the husband is only liable to a fine, and to be liable to this he must have kept his concubine under the conjugal roof. When taken in the very act of adultery with a married woman, the man can be punished on the complaint of the outraged husband, as the accomplice of the married woman; but his own wife has no right to prosecute him criminally, she can only seek a divorce. The murder of an adulterous wife or of her accomplice taken by a husband in the very act under the conjugal roof is *excusable*, but the murder of a husband by a wife under the same circumstances is *not excusable* according to the strict letter of the law, though a jury frequently corrects this legal inequality by acquitting the betrayed wife who has righted herself.

Again, the civil responsibility of the man and woman, whether they are married or unmarried, towards their natural children is not the same. The illegitimate child may claim his mother by legal proceedings, may sue her for maintenance as if he were legitimate, whilst he is forbidden to seek after his father, for fear of scandals that such quest would provoke. The legislator evidently thought that a woman, against whom a claim of this sort was made before the tribunals, would suffer less in her honour than a man put in the dock, or that the woman's honour was of less value than the man's honour. This rule was introduced into the Code at the demand of Napoleon, who on this occasion gave vent to an expression, which is still celebrated, on the little importance that ought to be attached to the act of a man who has been responsible for launching into the world an illegitimate child.

On account of her pecuniary interests, the married woman may be said to be under the perpetual tutelage of her husband, and this less for the purpose of increasing his importance than of protecting her against her own imprudence, for the legislator seems to have completely shared the ideas of the ancient jurists on "the imprudence, the frailty, and the imbecility" of woman. Accordingly, the law forbids her to dispose of her fortune or to defend her interests before the tribunals without her husband's approval. She cannot on her own authority bring an action or defend herself in a suit brought against her. Without her husband's consent the wife cannot make over, alienate, mortgage, or acquire any property. She cannot even receive gifts unless authorised by her husband, so that in strict accordance with the law, a letter of credit or a postal order cannot be delivered to a wife without her husband's leave. The husband's authority must be given for each occasion specially. He cannot give her a general authority once for all, either by the marriage contract or subsequently thereto, to alienate her realty; such an authority is null and void. Nor is of any value a consent given in ratification of an act done by the wife. Even the husband's decease will not prevent the act of the wife being null and void. In default of the husband's authority, the wife must obtain the leave of the court.

Thus, the married woman is absolutely precluded from disposing freely of her property for ever. So far as regards the management and enjoyment of her property, they only belong to her, in a greater or less degree, by virtue of an express stipulation in the marriage contract.

The French law distinguishes four different kinds of matrimonial arrangements, that is to say, there are four categories of provisions which rule the property relations of married persons: (1) community of property; (2) exclusion of such community; (3) separation of property; (4) the dower arrangement.

If the married persons have made no contract, property brought in by the wife becomes common property, and from that moment the husband becomes master of her fortune; he alone manages the property, and he can sell, alienate and mortgage it without his wife's consent. However, an exception is made as to real property brought in at the time of marriage or subsequently acquired by gift or inheritance. Such property is the *personal* property of husband or wife, as opposed to their common property. The husband cannot alienate the *personal* property of his wife without her consent, but he is always the person to manage it. On the other hand, if the wife, duly authorised, sells some of her real property, she may not take the money to herself; it goes to the common fund administered by the husband, and is not restored to her before the dissolution of the matrimonial partnership. So that, under the rule of *community of property*, a woman keeps only the bare proprietorship even in her personal property, the management and enjoyment of this as well as of her property falling into the common fund, being entirely in the hands of the husband. The fact that certain real property of the wife is excluded from the husband's right of disposal, constitutes far less important a guarantee for the wife at the present time than it was considered at the time when the code was framed, because now very frequently the greater part of a fortune consists not of real property but of chattels, namely of funds. Though master of the common property, the husband is somewhat limited in his power of impoverishing it, to the detriment of his wife, *e.g.*, he may not dispose *inter vivos* gratuitously of the common real property, nor bequeath by will a larger part of the common property than his own portion. The husband can avail himself of the common property to meet his liabilities, or may spend it in any other way for his personal use, but in all such cases he becomes liable for the refund of that property, which is to be effected at the dissolution of the matrimonial partnership. This dissolution takes place on account of death, divorce, legal separation of the parties, etc. And then, each of the parties or their respective heirs receives back all the personal property that he or she brought in, whilst the common property, after deduction of the refunds and compensations which the parties may owe one another, is divided between them in halves, whatever may have been the share of each at the time of marriage.

Such is the *legal* system which is applied in the absence of a contract, or where the parties declare at the time of the marriage that they are marrying under the rule of community of property. But the parties are at liberty to modify these rules by special arrangements in the marriage contract; they can stipulate that community of property shall include only property acquired by the parties collectively or separately during the marriage; they can exclude the chattels either in whole or in part; they can establish a complete community in all property present or future; they can assign unequal shares to either party in the common property, etc., etc.; in a word, they can regulate the common property at their pleasure, without, however, interfering with the general rule which forbids the married woman to dispose of her property or to sue in law without her husband's consent.

The parties can stipulate that they are marrying *without community of property.* In this case the husband has not the right to alienate or to pledge the property of his wife as under the rule of *community of property,* but it is always he who manages the whole of her fortune and enjoys the income from it. It can, however, be arranged that the wife should receive annually for her own maintenance and personal wants a certain portion of her income singly on her receipt.

In order that the wife may administer and freely enjoy her property and her income, the marriage contract must stipulate for *separation of property.* In this case each party on principle retains the rights which he or she had over the property before the marriage. The wife manages her property herself and enjoys her own income, but she cannot alienate her real property nor give away her chattels without the consent of her husband, or failing him, without the sanction of a court of justice. She needs likewise this consent or sanction to defend her property before the courts, according to the general rule which places the woman under the power of her husband.

To complete the protection which the law thought necessary to grant to a wife, in disposing of her property, against her own incompetence and "imbecility", the Code established yet a fourth matrimonial arrangement, termed *dotal.* Under this system the real property brought in by the wife and "assigned as her dowry" cannot be alienated nor mortgaged by the wife or by the husband, even both agreeing thereto, unless the marriage contract authorised it. In the absence of such a general authority given in advance, the *dotal* property may be disposed of only in a few exceptional cases expressly provided by the law. The rule of the inalienability of the dotal real property is for the purpose of preserving intact the wife's fortune and of preventing such cases as those, in which the wife under her husband's influence might be induced to allow him to alienate her property and thus imperil the prospects of her family. The management of dotal property is vested in the husband. He receives also and spends at his discretion all the income of it. He has to defray the charges of the household with that income; but if he manages to save a part of it, it becomes his own; if he invests these savings in property, this property is his. However, it can be stipulated by the marriage contract that the wife should receive for her own use a certain portion of her income, singly on her receipt. The dotal system does not require that all the fortune should be settled as dower, that is, made inalienable; the wife who marries under the *dotal* rule can reserve a portion of her property as her *paraphernalia,* over which she has a right of property, management and enjoyment, just as under the rule of *separation of property,* that is to say, always without prejudice to the rule which subjects the wife to her husband's authority for the purpose of alienating the property or of suing in law on account of it. The wife who has *paraphernalia* property reserved for her use, is bound, as in the case of complete *separation of property*, to contribute to the charges of the household, whilst under the rule of joint property, or of the dotal system, they are to be met by the husband alone, who in these cases has the full use of his wife's fortune.

The law secures the wife certain guarantees for the recovery of her property after the dissolution of the marriage; she has a legal lien (without any formal mortgage) on the real property of her husband, and, if the parties were married under the rule of *community of property*, her personal property is deducted from the husband's realty and chattels previously to other liens. If the common property is insufficient to answer the wife's claim, she may recover from the personal property of the husband, whilst the husband can only recover against the common property. But these guarantees are efficacious only in case the husband possesses a sufficient personal fortune. If he has no fortune, he may irreparably and with impunity imperil his wife's fortune. Under the rule of *community of property* he may dissipate his wife's property and reduce her to misery. Under the rules of the other matrimonial systems, which give him the use of his wife's income, he may employ it in unfortunate speculations, or even to satisfy his own pleasures or vices. In all such cases, when the wife's fortune is endangered, she may apply to the courts for a *separation of property*, for the purpose of taking from the husband the management and the use of her property. But perhaps that will come too late.

If the wife strives to get a livelihood by her own exertions to provide for herself and her family, she is still under her husband's thumb. The wife who is not separate in estate is not legally mistress of her earnings; they are regarded, like the rest of her income, as intended to defray the charges of the household, and are managed by the husband. The wife cannot carry on any trade unless authorised by him. If she has obtained his consent, she can bind herself, so far as concerns her trade, without the husband's authority; she can also, within that limit, pledge, mortgage or alienate her real property.

The recent law (of 1881) on Postal Savings Banks enlarged the civil capacity of married women, by authorising them, whatever might be the matrimonial arrangement, to deposit money in the banks and to take it out again without the assistance of their husbands, but in the latter case with the reserve that the husband may offer opposition if he thinks fit.

The married woman cannot obtain her emancipation otherwise than by the dissolution of the marriage; as soon as the marriage is dissolved, the woman, who up to that time was considered incapable of managing her own affairs, becomes suddenly capable of disposing of her property, suing in law, etc. Dissolution of marriage otherwise than by death of either husband or wife, or by condemnation to a penalty carrying with it civil death, was hardly possible before 1884. The law only allowed a *de facto* separation of husband and wife on his or her demand based on the grounds of adultery, cruelty, or serious injury inflicted by one on the other. This partial divorce, termed *separation of the body*, and obtained only by the way of legal proceedings, always involves separation of property. But the wife who was partially divorced did not recover all her civil capacity; to alienate or mortgage her property or to sue in law, she had to ask the consent of the husband from whom she was separated, or in default of it, to obtain leave of the court, which, as a matter of course, was never refused. A recent law of February, 1893, has restored to the partially divorced woman her civil capacity. In 1884, divorce, which existed under the Code Napoleon, and which was abolished in 1816 under the Royalist Restoration, was re-established; and now the woman, as well as the man, can obtain a definite divorce on all the grounds on which a partial divorce is allowed. Directly the divorce is pronounced the woman recovers her full civil capacity. As husband and wife are forbidden to change the matrimonial arrangement agreed to in the marriage contract, the legislator has thought it necessary to take precautions that this rule should not be evaded by means of a divorce. So the new law provides that, if divorced husbands and wives re-marry, they cannot make a matrimonial arrangement different from the settlement of their former alliance. The woman's power of contracting a new marriage after divorce is not the same as the man's; in the case of a divorce granted on the ground of adultery, the guilty wife can never marry the co-respondent, whilst as regards a guilty husband the law contains no similar prohibition.

The restoration of divorce, completed by the law of 1893 on partial divorce, has undoubtedly been a legislative measure of great importance to the woman. But the new emancipating law only indirectly affects her civil capacity, and that only in exceptional cases.

As soon as the divorced woman re-marries, she returns to the legal dependence that we have just considered. It is this dependence of the married woman which loudly calls for amendment. The account given of the laws in force for the time being is sufficient in itself to show the necessity and the justice of such a reform. Unfortunately, these laws have on their side the formidable protection of deeply-rooted social prejudices. Napoleon has said, "There is one thing that is not French, and that is, that a woman can do what she pleases." If at present, public opinion, I mean the public opinion of men, expresses itself on the subject less violently and less grittily, it is hardly less hostile to the extension of woman's rights and to the enlargement of her sphere of activity. Some timid attempts made in the French Parliament to do away with the restrictions on the civil capacity of women have come to nothing. A Bill, to grant women the right to be witnesses to deeds and to be guardians, though long since adopted by one of the two chambers, is still in abeyance. Other Bills, as, for example, proposals for doing away with the prohibition of the quest as to the fathership, have no chance of being adopted ; there are too many lawyers in the French chambers, who have been brought up in a superstitious and blunt respect for the Code Napoleon.

However, the cause of women's legal and social elevation progresses, though slowly. In this respect is especially noteworthy the progress made in the organisation for women's education. The university courses, though open to women, as has been stated above (see page 179), are within the reach only of a very select circle, and hitherto very few females have made up their minds to pass the threshold of the university lecture rooms, in the teeth of existing prejudices. Beneath the universities there were no public schools for young girls, where they might acquire general culture. The law of 27th December, 1880 (called the Camille Seé Law, after the deputy who was in charge of it), has filled up this wide gap, by establishing secondary education for girls similar to that which is given to boys in the *lycées*. Under the provisions of this law girls' *lycées* and colleges are established by the State, while the Départements and the Communes contribute to the expenses. The education given in those schools includes moral instruction, French, one foreign language at least, ancient and modern literature, geography and cosmography, the national history and a sketch of general history, arithmetic, the elements of geometry, chemistry, physics and natural history, hygiene, domestic economy, needlework, legal information pertaining to common life concerns, drawing, music and gymnastics. Religious teaching is given, at the request of parents, by the ministers of the different religions, in the school-rooms, but out of school hours. Every *lycée* or college is placed under the authority of a directress. The professors are men or women who hold regular diplomas. To enable women professors to qualify themselves, a Higher Normal school for the secondary education of girls was opened in 1881. M. Ernest Legouvé, the eminent academician, and one of the men who have earned the greatest credit in the cause of French female education, is at the head of this school. There is already a considerable number of female *lycées* and colleges, and they are working very successfully.

The organisation of this teaching has been a revolution,

the effects of which will be much further reaching than many people imagine. When a number of young girls, brought up in the *lycées*, enter society, its ideas will undergo an important, and, in my opinion, a beneficial change; the moral tone of women, and consequently of society in general, will be found to be elevated, and legislation itself will have to yield to the demand for modifications in favour of women. That this end will be obtained more quickly or obtained at all by the way of claiming for women political rights is hardly possible. The agitation for female suffrage, which, in France, has not yet passed out of the domain of the ridiculous, is likely, in the present state of French opinion, only to compromise the just claims of women in the sphere of civil law, and cannot but foster and strengthen the deplorable prejudices which exist in France against admitting woman to a place outside the alcove and the *salon*.

§ 2.

The French Civil Code, introduced, under Napoleon, into several other countries which were then under the supremacy of France, retained the force of law in those countries, with or without modifications. So in *Belgium* and *Holland*, the civil capacity of woman is still regulated by the French provisions, which we have just examined.

The *Italian* Code, on the contrary, has introduced into Napoleonic legislation some very important changes, namely in regard to the legal condition of the married woman. Whilst maintaining for the husband the management of the wife's property, and whilst forbidding her to alienate or mortgage her realty, to contract loans, or to sue in law on account of such property, without her husband's consent, Italian law allows the husband to give his wife a general power of attorney for all such acts, or a special power of attorney for some. This authority is revocable, but, so far as it goes, the married woman is in full possession of her civil capacity. In this way the Italian husband is able legally to emancipate his wife by a public act, while the French husband can give his wife a general authority only to manage her own property. Apart from the general authority of the husband, which is optional, Italian law dispenses the wife from the necessity of obtaining the approval by her husband or the court in several cases: when she transacts commercial business on her own account; when she is legally separated from her husband through his fault; when the husband is under age or under an interdict, or is an absentee; or when he is serving his time in prison. Thanks to this, the Italian woman has far more frequently than in France a free hand, although she may not be emancipated by her husband. In Italy, matrimonial arrangements, which consist of community of property and the dower system, are much less rigid than in France. Community of property under Italian law cannot comprise all the property of husband and wife, but is confined to property acquired during coverture, and even in respect to this limited category of common property, the husband can only alienate or mortgage it for a consideration; he cannot dispose of it gratuitously as he can in France, and so the power of the husband to squander his wife's fortune is diminished. The Italian system of dower differs from the French in this, that the principle of the inalienability of dotal property is not absolute. It may be disposed of with the consent of the husband or the authority of the court, and in this way can be frequently obviated the inconvenience attached to the dotal system, which immobilizes the dowry, and narrows thereby the economical activity of the country, to which dotal fortunes might contribute. Lastly, after the dissolution of marriage, the dowry is liable for debts contracted by the wife during coverture, so that the dowry turns into an engine of credit for the woman, that is to say into a means of acting, of asserting her personality.

The *Spanish* laws regarding the civil capacity of women resemble very closely the provisions of the French Code. There have been, however, some more liberal provisions introduced into the former. Thus, the duty of the wife to follow her husband wherever he chooses to live is no longer absolute, as it is under the Code Napoleon; the Spanish courts can exempt the wife from this obligation if the husband settles beyond the seas or in foreign countries. The wife separated from her husband in estate need not, in order to dispose of her real property, first ask the consent of her husband, but may apply direct to the court; whilst in France, up to 1893, the woman separated from a husband even after legal proceedings, and being in consequence at warfare with her husband, was nevertheless obliged to apply to him first every time she wanted to exert her right to dispose of her property. But as divorce is not recognised in Spain any more than it is in Italy, the wife cannot recover her complete civil capacity during her husband's life-time. The only resource open to her is a separation of person, which for the wife does not always mean a separation of property. If, by the sentence pronouncing the separation, judgment has been given against the wife, she has, in Spain, no right to anything but alimony, and her husband retains the management and use of her property, whilst the husband, if found guilty, does not forfeit the management of his own property.

§ 3.

The Code Napoleon served as a basis of civil legislation in the French-speaking cantons of *Switzerland, i.e.*, Geneva, Vaud, Fribourg, Neufchâtel, etc. The other cantons escaped this influence, but the legal condition of woman has not on that score been more favourable in the German cantons. The ancient customs and laws of the Middle Ages, which maintained themselves there, kept woman in a state of complete dependence, not only as regards her property, but also with regard to her person. Up to 1881, in several cantons a woman, whether married or unmarried, a spinster or a widow, was looked upon as being perpetually under age and subject to tutelage. The federal statute, of 1881, on civil capacity, substituting one uniform law for the special cantonal provisions on the subject, raised women from this degrading position; every restriction of civil capacity in general, on account of sex, is removed, but persons of full age may voluntarily submit themselves to a guardian or curator, in order the better to safeguard their interests. The right of succession, regulated by cantonal legislation, allows a distinction between the two sexes; sometimes the sons take a larger share than the daughters; sometimes the sons are preferred to the daughters in the succession to real property, and sometimes maternal relatives competing for the inheritance with paternal relatives have to give way to them. The condition of married women is also determined differently by the different cantonal laws. The husband's authority over his wife's person is generally expressed in the severe language of the ancient codes, but it is no longer unqualified; thus the duty of a wife to follow her husband is not absolute. Even among the laws of the French-speaking group, which follow the Code Napoleon, the law of Fribourg, whilst asserting the duty of the wife to follow her husband, adds, "as long as she has no serious motive for refusing to do so." In several German cantons expatriation of the husband or considerations of health, are, according to the law, sufficient reasons for such refusal. Compelling the wife to reside under the same roof as her husband is no longer customary, although the laws of certain cantons contain penalties for the non-cohabitation of husband and wife.

The rule of matrimonial property in Switzerland is again far from favourable to the wife. In several cantons it is even less liberal than that of the Code Napoleon. Thus there is no liberty of matrimonial contracts; the legal system, which, under the French Code and the laws of the Swiss-French cantons, is only subsidiary, is in the other cantons the obligatory rule, and it is but little respectful of the wife's rights. In the single canton of Tessin the legal rule is *separation of property;* in the others it is sometimes based on the *union of property,* where the husband has the management and the use of his wife's fortune, and sometimes on the *unity of property*, where all the property brought in by the wife becomes the full property of the husband, under the obligation for him to restore its value to the wife at the dissolution of the marriage. In several cantons these different systems are more or less combined. Federal legislation has only intervened for the purpose of enlarging the civil capacity of women carrying on a trade. It did so by providing that the married woman, who, with the express or implied authority of her husband, exercises any profession or trade, may contract for all her property on account of such profession or trade, whatever may be the husband's rights of management or use over such property. The divorced woman recovers her complete civil capacity, but not the wife who is separated in bed and board. But withal, divorce is made easier in Switzerland than in France. Since 1874, it can be pronounced there, to whatever religious denomination the parties may belong, at their request made on the ground that a continuance of their married life is incompatible with the nature of marriage; whilst in France the mutual consent of husband and wife is not a sufficient ground for granting them a divorce.

§ 4.

The civil laws of the several German States are about to be consolidated in a single code for the whole German Empire. Without, therefore, examining in detail the numerous codes, which will be annulled before long, I will simply point out the chief features of the legal condition of the German woman, paying a special attention to the Prussian provisions on the subject. The two principal matrimonial rules there are *union of property* and *community of property*. Under the first rule all the property brought in by the wife comes under the power of the husband. The husband works and leases the real property, and receives the interest derived from capital as well as the income from the trade or industry carried on by his wife. Any debt incurred by her is considered null and void. But, along with the property *brought* to the husband, the law allows woman to possess, in full proprietary right, certain property *reserved* for that purpose. The matrimonial contract can include in such *reserved* property every kind of property, realty or chattels, and the wife can dispose of it absolutely, mortgage, or even alienate it without her husband's consent. All the income accruing from such property, as well as the profits of industry or trade carried on by the woman by means of such property, are equally her own. If she makes a bad use of her income to such an extent that she becomes liable to the charge of extravagance, the husband can obtain from the proper court the appointment of a *curator*, as is done in the case of spendthrifts generally. Thus, under this only restriction, the wife may emancipate herself from the power of her husband by stipulating for *reserved* property. It is not impossible to do this even after marriage, for the law allows changes to be made in marriage contracts, and property *brought in* to be changed to property *reserved*, or *vice versâ*.

Community of property, if not obligatory under

the provincial laws, can be arranged by mutual agreement. It may be complete or confined to property acquired by husband and wife during coverture. If there are in the contract no distinct provisions as to the community of property, it is understood, contrary to the French rule, that the community of property extends only to acquired property. The husband manages and uses the common property, but he cannot without the wife's consent part with her realty or capital invested in her name. Even his right to dispose of her chattels can be challenged by the wife; she can object to donations *inter vivos*, which would curtail the common property to such an extent as to hazard her recovery of what she had *brought in*, should a dissolution of the marriage take place; and she may do this even if it was not stipulated for in the marriage contract.

This system, which is a great advance on the French Code, is about to be made still more favourable to women by the new Civil Code of the Empire; in fact, the draft scheme of this code extends the contractual capacity of the married woman, and secures her the profits made in carrying on a trade or profession. It also proposes to allow women to be testamentary witnesses.

In *Austria* the legal condition of the wife leaves little to be desired. The legal rule, that is to say, the rule which is applied in the absence of matrimonial contracts, is the complete *separation of property*, husband and wife each keeping all the rights they possessed before marriage. The legal presumption is that the husband, as representative of the wife, manages her fortune, but only so long as the wife does not object. Even if the wife expressly and for ever entrusted the management to the husband, it can be withdrawn from him if there is reason to fear for the safety of her property. In the same way the husband can intervene in the case of his wife's bad management of her fortune, and get her declared a spendthrift. The dowry brought by the wife benefits the husband; if it is in money, it becomes his full property; but if it consists of land, the husband enjoys only the income. Community of property is not obligatory, but it can be stipulated for in the marriage contract. If the wife's fortune is endangered from being in the husband's hands, she may obtain a legal separation, which is open to all, while divorce is granted only to non-Catholics.

§ 5.

In the *Scandinavian* countries important changes have taken place in the legal condition of the wife during the last twenty years. Under the rule of the old Swedish Code of 1734, spinsters, though of age, always remained under tutelage unless they obtained a dispensation from the king. The law of 1884 declared every unmarried woman of twenty-one years to be of full age and capable of managing and disposing of her property herself. If she wishes to renounce the benefit of her majority, she must make a declaration before the court, which then places her under tutelage (as in Switzerland). In 1864 the same change was introduced into Finland, where the Swedish Code of 1734 remained in force, after it became a Russian dependency. The civil capacity of married women has also been enlarged in Sweden by recent legislation in the direction of separation of fortunes and liberty of matrimonial contracts. The married woman can, now, keep for herself the management of her own property and sue in law on account of such property. Until quite recently female rights of succession were not the same in the country as they were in the towns. Whilst in the latter, women had equal shares with sons, they obtained only a third share of the inheritance in the country. The law of May 16, 1890, has abolished this privilege of the sons.

In Norway, the property relations of husband and wife have been recently rearranged by the law of 1888. In principle the married woman has the same capacity as the unmarried woman. Both husband and wife manage their own property, while common property is managed by the husband alone. Yet he cannot give away a tenth part of it gratuitously, without the consent of his wife. This consent is equally necessary if the husband wishes to alienate, mortgage, or lease real property situated in the country and brought into the common fund by the wife. Even under the rule of *community of property* the wife has the full right to dispose of what she earns by personal industry as well as of all acquisitions made out of her earnings.

Denmark only obtained this last reform (which gives the wife the power to dispose of the profits of her industry) in 1880. In other matters the husband's power over the person as well as over the property of the wife has maintained its old rigour. The legal matrimonial rule is *community of property*, and all the property and income of the wife falls into the common fund. The husband is looked upon as guardian of his wife in respect of all her rights and acts. Even the unmarried woman, whatever her age may be, remains in a state of minority and tutelage.

§ 6.

Russia, on the contrary, whose political institutions are the least liberal in Europe, possesses most liberal laws as regards the civil capacity of women. Every woman of age, whether married or unmarried, enjoys in Russia full civil capacity. There is not in Russian law any legal system of matrimonial property arrangements. Marriage does not in any way change the rights of husband and wife over the fortunes they possess or may acquire; the husband has no legal power over his wife's fortune; she can acquire, alienate, bind herself or sue in law, just as any person of full age, without asking anyone's permission. This absolute *separation of property* is not always upheld in reality, for Russian husbands and wives generally live as under the rule of *community of property*, but it is so of their own free will, and they can always change. The husband's marital power consists solely in his right to require the wife to cohabit with him; but if, for example, the parties occupy a house belonging to the wife, there is nothing to prevent her legally evicting the husband, whilst he is free to compel her to follow him to his new domicile. The only disability to which women are subjected with respect to their civil capacity is in regard to their right of succession. Daughters do not inherit intestate property in equal shares with sons; each daughter obtains one-fourteenth of the realty and one-seventh of the chattels, and then the remainder, after the deduction of the widow's share, is divided equally between the sons. But if the legal shares of the daughters do not leave, at least, an equal amount for the sons, the property is equally divided between all the children.